湛庐文化
Cheers Publishing
a mindstyle business
与 思 想 有 关

65

Successful
HARVARD BUSINESS SCHOOL
Application Essays

引言

展现真实的自己

我们无法保证，你买了这本书就一定能进哈佛商学院。的确，经常有书籍或网站声称他们可以做到这一点，但我们不保证。想必，这也是你选择这本书的原因之一：我们有一说一，实话实说。

本书既不是录取之路的直通车，也没有什么诀窍可以助你过关斩将。然而，本书会激发你的灵感，让你写出优秀的Essay；它会告诉你，所谓的万能答案是不存在的。哈佛商学院作为世界顶尖商学院，是一个精彩纷呈、极富多元化的地方，平均每90名学生会来自近30个不同的国家。除了地理上的多样性，这里的学生还有银行家、咨询师、医生、律师、飞行员、教师、作家和运动员等各种身份。因此，本书精选的Essay主题广泛，写作风格迥异，希望能以此展现哈佛商学院学生群体的高度国际化和多样性。我们的目的是，通过推荐各种成功入选的范文，揭开录取流程的神秘面纱。每个命题可以有多种回答角度，而我们只是提供一个成功的案例。所谓的万能答案就是没有万能答案。做你自己，实话实说，深思熟虑。展现真实的自己以及你处理问题的方式，告诉录取委员会，是什么塑造了现在的你。

乍看之下，你可能觉得自己并不那么优秀，无法从一群申请人中脱颖而出，毕竟，哈佛商学院平均每年会收到9 000多份申请。本书收录的范文，希望能帮你打消此类顾虑。尽管有些 Essay 的主题取材于申请人某段令人惊叹的经历，但大多数 Essay 的主题都取材于日常生活，甚至是些琐碎杂事。但即使这些申请人做普通的工作，也会用一种与众不同的方式表达。关键是，你要明白，那些奇闻轶事从来都不是结果，而是用以传达你的性格、价值观、自我认知、成熟度、领导技能、幽默感等能帮你在商学院大展拳脚的工具。即使是最异乎寻常的成就，如果没能在 Essay 中阐明你从中学到了什么、你发生了哪些改变，以及它为什么重要，那么这篇文章也是无效的。反之，那些看上去不值一提的活动，比如晨跑、坐出租车时的见闻等，也能成为理想的素材，用来展现你个性中的关键特点，或者用来解释你为何树立这样的人生目标。

如果你静心思考所有那些塑造和影响过你的经历，你可能会找到比写 Essay 所需素材多得多的东西。理想状态下，你可以把它们全部写进 Essay 里，但是考虑到篇幅有限，需要挑出最重要的部分。列一个清单（即使只是在头脑中简单规划一下），然后开始构思 6~7 篇作文。虽然有一些“万金油”式的主题可以回答全部的申请命题，但每一个故事都应该引出一个关于“你”的独特见解：你的思考方式和处世方式，你的家庭、职业，以及你的教育（包括但不限于此）。由于篇幅有限，每一个字都很宝贵，所以千万不要重复。例如，你在其中一篇 Essay 中展示了自己作为管理者的才干，那么就该在下一篇 Essay 中介绍一段有深度的私人经历，比如与兄弟姐妹的关系等。你展现的性格维度越广，录取委员会就越能更好地认识你。你的最终任务是尽可能多地展示简历、成绩单和 GMAT 分数所无法表现的那个你。虽然刚才提到的那些因素也很重要，但是 Essay 写作给了你一个表现机会，来展示自己能成为为哈佛商学院团体作出贡献的强者，并远不限于此。

一旦你构思好了 Essay 的大致内容，就要面对另一个障碍：字数限制。是否真的能用短短 300 个单词进行深入的剖析？读完本书范文，你将确信无疑。实际上，300 个单词提供了足够的篇幅来展现你自己。我们建议你在打草稿时就当没有字数限制，随性发挥，然后再来删掉冗余的文字（当然，并不是只有这个办法）。整个过程会逼着你不断追问自己：“我到底想表达什么？我的核心信息是什么？”这样，你就能剔除冗余的描述和不相关的细节，最终完成一篇简洁清晰、主题集中的好作文。

另外请记住，你是在给商学院写 Essay。如果你的文字优美，当然是锦上添花，但是别为此彻夜不眠。内容好，才是真的好！

最后提醒一句，绝对不要抄袭本书中的范文，你甚至不该把它们作为你在写作文时的模板或纲要。剽窃的作文必然会被发现，你的努力也就打了水漂。你很忙，录取委员会的成员也很忙，不要浪费你的时间，同时也别浪费他们的。

从阅读这 65 篇经典 Essay 开始吧。我们 *Harbus* 编辑部的资深编辑们为每篇作文撰写了精彩的点评，相信你在读过之后，一定大有收获。我们认为，它们是优秀的范文，但它们也仅仅是范文。它们反映了你的文章需要作出的反思和应该达到的深度。为了完成一篇有效的 Essay，你需要书写你自己。所以，深吸一口气，放松下来（这可能不容易），然后书写出你作为一名独特候选人的故事！

祝你好运！

丹·埃尔克　帕韦尔·斯威特克

哈佛商学院 2004 届 MBA

哈佛商学院 *Harbus* 新闻传媒公司代表

65

Successful
HARVARD BUSINESS SCHOOL
Application Essays

目录

BEING A LEADER

命题 1
领导经历

Choose a recent experience in which you acted as a leader. Briefly outline the situation, describe your leadership role, and then explain how you were effective and what you learned.

Discuss an experience that has had an impact on your development as a leader.

选取你最近一次作为领导者的经历。简要介绍当时情况，描述你作为领导者的任务，并说明你如何胜任这一工作，以及从中学到的经验教训。

讲述一段影响你领导能力形成、发展的经历。

解题思路

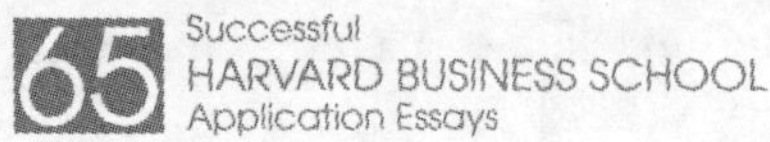

在构思该命题之前，你必须先形成自己的领导力概念。领导力不等于基本管理技能，也不等于发号施令。事实上，你越深入思考，就越难给出一个唯一的定义。在回顾自己的生活经历时，你会发现，领导技能体现在各种情境下，并且形式多样。

下面几篇范文就体现了这种多样性。例如，有些申请人认为，领导力体现在团队合作中；有些申请人认为，领导力体现在领导组织进行的变革中；甚至其中一篇范文提到，领导力表现为迅速决断下属的去留。

许多申请人难以提炼自己的领导经历。对于大多数工作时间还不长的大学毕业生而言，没做过《财富》500强公司的部门主管，或未曾根治亚马孙河流域的某种疾病并不奇怪，也是预料之中的情况。然而，领导力并不需要多么宏大的场景。下面几篇范文将告诉你：日常军事训练所提供的展示领导力的机会和一家大学校报提供的一样多；与学校院系交涉可能和协调非洲的一个跨国项目，或者说服一家公司调整产品研发方向一样充满挑战性。

这个命题的目的，不是让你胡乱编出一段添油加醋的文字，把某个大项目的功劳都归在自己名下，而是让你描述一段经历——它的结局因你的想法和行为而改写。但是，结果本身并不重要，重要的是你从中学到的东西。也许领导力难以界定，但是锻炼个人领导力却要在不断地自我剖析中加以学习。你精心挑选的事例，需要强调的正是这种能力。为了让读者留下深刻、持久的印象，文章应该清楚地说明你对领导力概念的理解、你如何在实践中加以运用，以及你认为应如何提高这项难以捉摸的技能。

点评人：帕韦尔·斯威特克（Pawel Swiatek）

01
组建团队以诚为本

There are over ten million children orphaned by HIV/AIDS living in sub-Saharan Africa. I met several last year during my visit to Gaborone, Botswana—Phangisilie, Grace, and Joseph to name but a few. They, along with the other four hundred children at the Mpule Kwelegobe Center for Children, will at least have access to care as a result of the efforts of an unlikely collaboration between businesspeople and artists whom I led over a six-month period.

I joined Bristol-Myers Squibb (BMS) to serve as an international project manager on Secure the Future, a $100 million five-year program that provides care and support for women and children with HIV/AIDS in five southern African countries, primarily through grants for medical research and community education. Among my first assignments was raising awareness and mobilizing resources for AIDS victims by using art. Developing a team of over thirty individuals from BMS, several African art galleries and museums, and our South African-based communications firm, we partnered with the Harvard AIDS Institute and the former Miss Universe, Mpule Kwelegobe, to create ArtWorks for AIDS. The exhibition included original commissioned pieces from more than thirty artists on the subject of HIV/AIDS, emphasizing the plight of women and children. ArtWorks premiered at the World Conference on AIDS in Durban just six months after it was conceived, toured several international venues, and earned close to $100,000 for AIDS orphans during an auction on November 30.

As the international project manager-leader, I was responsible for devising a vision and strategy for the project, assembling the team, establishing milestones, maintaining the budget, and delivering the art by the beginning of July. I was effective in this role

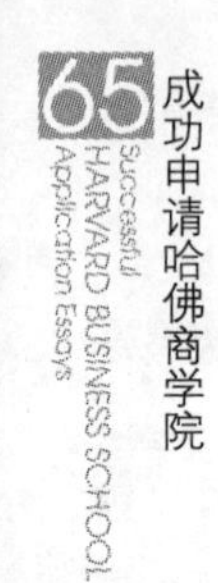

for several reasons. First, I ensured that the team, rather than I alone, collectively devised a vision and timeline for the project by meeting with the key participants individually to better understand their ideas. We then conducted a brainstorming session where all involved parties freely expressed their ideas to the group. Thus, each team member could claim ownership in our success. Second, I was able to mitigate cultural differences between the southern African, northern European, and American participants because of my extensive study of and travel to both regions. Third, although I recognized that the team members from the art community did not necessarily subscribe to business principles, I never let them use it as an excuse for poor performance.

My key learning is somewhat simple but compelling nonetheless; anytime you create a team comprising parties who are naturally suspicious of one another, honesty is paramount. That's the only way I could get artists to trust and perform for businessmen and vice versa. I fostered this sense of trust by maintaining clear lines of communication between all parties as well as refusing to alter the mutually agreed upon project tenants just to suit the interests of whomever I was speaking with. The result was a stunning visual homagc to the over twenty-four million people suffering from HIV/AIDS in Africa as well as additional care and support for hundreds of children in Botswana. But why don't you see for yourself…the Smithsonian purchased two of the works.

点评

阅读完这篇文章，你可能忍不住揣测，正是申请人在文中描述的项目——其值得称颂的、突出的人道主义性质，奠定了本文成功的基础，但事实并非如此。尽管参与艾滋病社区关怀项目这件事表明申请人投身世界发展事业，其精神令人敬佩，但这本身并不足以说明他的领导能力。申请人着力描述项目的来龙去脉以表现它的重要性，但接下来用了更大篇幅叙述自己作为项目领导人所面临的挑战，以及为克服困难所采用的解决办法。

协作、建立共识、弥合文化差异在其他情境下听起来是模糊的抽象概念，在此处却是申请人领导力才能的具体表现——带领一支文化多元、背景各异的跨国队伍。申请人向录取委员会展示了自己的才能，并没有言过其实。也许，增加一两个简短但有说服力的趣闻（同时缩减背景描述）会使他的叙述更具活力。

本文结尾是点睛之笔。申请人表示，此次项目也是一次学习的机会。以后，无论领导何种项目，他都会将培养参与者之间的信任以及创造开放的沟通环境置于首位。可以肯定，这将会使他成为更有效的领导者。

【参考译文】

在撒哈拉沙漠以南的非洲地区，有上千万儿童因为艾滋病变成了孤儿。去年，我在博茨瓦纳的哈博罗内[①]访问期间，遇见了潘吉、格雷斯、约瑟夫等孤儿。他们连同姆普勒·克维拉格博儿童中心其余的 400 名孩子一起，得到了应有的照料，而这是一群几乎不可能合作的商人和艺术家通力协作的结果。我作为一名领导者，领导他们长达 6 个月的时间。

我曾加入百时美施贵宝公司（BMS），担任“保障未来”计划的一名跨国项目经理。“保障未来”是一个为期 5 年，耗资 1 亿美元的计划，主要通过资助医学研究和社区教育的方式，在 5 个非洲南部国家为感染艾滋病病毒的妇女、儿童提供援助关怀。我最初的任务，是利用艺术创作提高大众对艾滋病患者的认识，并为艾滋病患者募集资源。我们同哈佛艾滋病研究所和前环球小姐姆普勒·克维拉格博合作，组建了一个 30 多人的团队，创作表现艾滋病的艺术品。团队成员分别来自 BMS 公司、若干家非洲艺术画廊和博物馆，以及我们驻扎在南非的联络处。展览的艺术品包括 30 多位艺术家的原创作品，均以艾滋病为主题，突出展现妇女、儿童的遭遇。项目成立后仅 6 个月，这些艺术品就在德班举行的世界艾滋病大会上首次亮相，并在一些国际场合巡回展出。11 月 30 日的拍卖会还为艾滋病孤儿筹集了约 10 万美元。

作为该项目的管理者和领导者，我负责为该项目制订远景战略，组织团队成员，设定阶段性目标，控制预算，并确保在7月初递交作品。我的工作卓有

① 博茨瓦纳是非洲南部的一个内陆国，哈博罗内是该国的首都。——译者注

成效，理由有如下几条。第一，我与团队中的重要成员逐个面谈，更好地理解他们的想法，确保了团队，而不是我个人，共同为这个项目制订远景目标和时间表。我们还进行了一次头脑风暴会议，会议上，所有与会人员自由表达对这个集体的想法。这样一来，每位成员都为项目的成功增添了一份力量。第二，我能够减少来自非洲南部、欧洲北部以及美国的队员们之间的文化差异，因为我曾多次前往非洲南部和欧洲北部，并对这两个地区进行了大量研究。第三，虽然我明白那些搞艺术的成员不一定认同商业原则，但是，我从不让他们以此作为自己表现欠佳的借口。

我的收获有点简单，但令人信服：当你组建一个团队时，各方之间难免存在猜疑，以诚为本是最重要的。这也是我让艺术家信任商人并为之工作的唯一办法，也是让商人相信艺术家并与之共事的唯一办法。我时刻保持各方之间沟通渠道的畅通，同时，不管谈判对象是谁，我绝不因任何单方面的利益而修改先前共同达成的协议，这两点促进了团队之间的信任。最终，我们将作品以令人惊叹的视觉表现手法，献给2 400万名艾滋病患者；同时，博茨瓦纳的数百名儿童获得了额外的生活保障。亲眼去看看吧，史密森尼博物院购买了其中的两件作品呢！

02

让不同利益群体通力协作

As managing editor of University of Michigan's student newspaper, I was responsible for deciding how to appropriately cover the football team's quest for its first national championship in over fifty years. I decided to publish a special edition on the afternoon of Michigan's final regular season game—but only if the team won. As managing editor, I led a team of reporters, editors, advertising managers, and circulation managers that successfully printed the first Saturday afternoon edition in the 107-year history of the *Michigan Daily*.

My greatest challenge was to align the separate staffs in one common vision. While the editorial staff was excited about the project, many advertising managers felt uncomfortable selling ads for a newspaper that may never get published. Likewise, the circulation department had qualms about distributing the newspapers when university buildings, our usual delivery points, were closed. I met with the leaders of each staff to discuss their concerns and gain a greater understanding of their operations. I evaluated various scenarios, and developed a plan in which editorial and business staffs would collaborate on circulation and advertising responsibilities. This not only alleviated concerns about a tight deadline, but also allowed sportswriters and advertising managers to collectively identify local merchants that would covet advertising space in this issue. Additionally, the circulation department worked with the arts and leisure staff to select local bars and restaurants as new delivery points.

Through this experience I learned to integrate disparate inputs into a unified perspective. Although very little can be accomplished without well-balanced, multi-disciplined teams, molding different viewpoints into a single vision is a task that can trip up all but the most successful leaders. I've learned to request input from each

team member, not because it is important to make them feel valuable, but because open discussion is the best way to generate successful ideas.

点 评

申请人在讲述自己的领导经历时，突出了其中一个最大的挑战，也是任何一个机构的领导者都要面对的挑战，即如何让利益不同的人通力协作。申请人给出了足够的细节来描述问题的复杂性：从广告销售到报纸派送，每一位参与这个开创性、非传统项目的团队成员有着数不清的担忧。毋庸置疑，出版首份周末特刊绝非轻而易举的事情，它需要申请人使出浑身解数，通过谈判达成共识。

不过，这篇文章之所以入选，并不单单因为申请人描述了一个富有远见的领导过程，或是他如何带领团队达成共识，完成了一个标志性的项目。这些要素都很重要，但还远远不够。这篇文章入选的原因是，申请人对这段领导经历的总结。申请人的才能不仅体现在他创办了一份大学校报的周末特刊上，更体现在他对如何管理及激励一个大团队的理解，而这一技能可以应用在比密歇根大学校刊更广阔的环境中。换言之，申请人展现了他在商业环境中的领导潜力。

假如本文变换一下叙述的顺序，可以锦上添花。如果以简略描述管理上面临的挑战开篇，会让文章更有动感，引起读者对事件背景以及解决办法的好奇心。与数千篇同主题的文章竞争时，一段抓人眼球的开篇能给你带来很大的优势。

【参考译文】

在我担任密歇根大学校刊执行总编期间，正赶上校橄榄球队 50 多年来第一次参加全国冠军争夺赛，我负责决策如何合宜地报道这场赛事。我决定在常规赛最后一场比赛的下午出版一份特刊——当然，前提必须是我们校队获胜。

作为执行总编，我领导记者、编辑、广告经理以及发行经理在内的一干人等成功出版发行了《密歇根日报》创刊 107 年以来首份周六下午版特刊。

我最大的挑战是让分工不同的团队成员共享一个愿景、目标。尽管编辑团队对于这个项目跃跃欲试，但许多广告经理并不太想为一份可能根本不会下印的报纸卖广告位。类似地，发行部门也对报纸的派送心存疑虑，因为当时我们日常的派送点——各学校大楼都关门了。我与各团队的负责人开会讨论他们的担忧，从而更好地理解他们的工作流程。我评估了各种情境，设计出一套方案，让编辑部门与营销部门合作，分担发行和广告业务。这不仅缓解了由于日程紧张所带来的困扰，还让体育记者和广告经理有机会一起发掘想要在此刊上刊登广告的本地商人。另外，发行部门也与美工部门合作，挑选了一些当地的酒吧和饭馆作为新的报纸派送点。

通过这次经历，我学会了如何把多股力量拧成一股。缺乏稳定和谐、训练有素的团队成不了大事，能让观点不一的员工齐心协力，也是成功的领导者必须拥有的能力。我学会了如何要求每位团队成员各尽其力，不仅仅是因为让每个人感觉到自身的价值是很重要的，也因为激发好点子的最佳途径是开诚布公地讨论。

03
谨慎计划确保成功

I was elected the first foreign chairman of the Oxford University engineering student board (ESB). My most difficult challenge was to convince the faculty to change the way our courses were taught. No former chairmen had attempted that successfully. Moreover, I had only one month to persuade them if changes were to be implemented for the following year. The curriculum assigned equal weighting and time to all courses. However, to learn effectively, we needed different time allocations. Politically, this was very sensitive, as faculty egos were at stake: more time might imply poor teaching and less time might imply less significance.

As I learned in organizational behavior classes, I appealed to the faculty rationally, emotionally, and through syndication. First, I led twenty committee members to carry out a comprehensive student survey. By working together, splitting the target group of 720 students between us, we achieved a record 80 percent response rate. Second, I focused the faculty, who were under pressure from the British government to improve teaching standards, on the bigger picture. I offered them a way to bring the students on board. Lastly, I spoke to all key faculty members, incorporated their feedback and briefed them on the results. Therefore, there were no surprises at the ESB meeting, the faculty accepted our recommendation, and it was implemented the following year.

I learned that with teamwork and individual accountability we accomplished a survey that decoupled the link between course importance and time allocation, which provided the most objective evidence for change. Emotionally, I empathized with the faculty and emphasized the need to improve our course. I compared us to other universities to avoid the personal "ego traps" within the department. Most importantly, syndication prior to the actual meeting ensured a successful conclusion.

点评

即使对官员来说，对组织中旧有的规范和程序进行革新都是一项艰巨的挑战。申请人对改革作出了颇具政治色彩的描述，使成功显得遥不可及。尽管如此，他严谨、全面、周到的领导风格为他创造了成功：领导学生进行民意调查，小心谨慎地向学院提出一个双赢的新方案。他不只是一个按部就班的管理者，更是一位沟通者。积极分析事件中各方的动机，厘清他们的理性动机和感性动机，这份理解力让他与众人达成共识，成功领导变革。

学院最终的同意似乎是申请人积极努力的必然结果，仿佛他早已计划妥当，从头到尾一个细节都不差。申请人把自己塑造成一位能干的领导，没有螳臂挡车，轻率地对抗学院；而是事先分析情势，制订详细的策略，然后领导其支持者共同努力，达成目标。文章确定无疑地展示了申请人具备制订目标、争取广泛的支持以及达成目标所需的领导技能。

尽管这篇 Essay 已经准确传达了申请人希望表达的观点，但若是能在结尾对经验教训的总结作进一步精炼会更好。“团队合作”和“个人的责任感”不足以反映申请人在实际工作中明确表现出来的对领导技能的深刻理解。总结若能更全面些，可使本文更出众。

【参考译文】

我曾当选为牛津大学工程学院学生会（ESB）的第一位外籍主席，遇到的最大的挑战是说服学院调整课程的教学方式。历任主席没有一位能够成功说服院方；更何况，要想在明年就实行新的教学安排，我只剩一个月的时间去说服他们。学院对所有科目安排了同样的学分和课时，可是我们需要不同的课时安排，才能提高学习效率。这是一件非常敏感的事情，是对学院权威的挑战：课时安排偏长，影射该科目老师的教学水平差；课时安排偏短，则可能意味着该科目不受重视。

根据组织行为学课堂上学习的内容，我有理有节地向学院提出申请，传达学生们的心声。首先，我带领 20 位学生会成员，开展了一次全面的学生民意调查。我们精诚合作，分别负责 720 位调查对象，创造了高达 80% 的回复率纪录。其次，更大的背景是，学院正受到来自英国政府要求其提高教学标准的压力。我提出让学生们共同参与行动。最后，我与学院每个关键人物沟通，听取他们的意见，并汇报调查结果。果不其然，在工程学院学生大会上，学院接受了我们的建议，并于第二年开始实施。

我认识到，是团队合作和个人责任感这两项因素帮助我们完成了这项调查，从而打破了课程重要性和课时分配两者之间的联系，为课程调整提供了最客观的证据。在情感方面，我表示愿与学院共进退，强调改善课程安排的必要性。我将我们学校与其他大学相比较，避开了院系老师内部个人化的“自我陷阱”。最重要的是，正式会议之前的学生联合组织确保了最后的成功。

04
面对制度抵制坚持不懈

Traditionally, investment banks perform exhaustive financial due diligence to understand a company's prospects before accepting it as a client. During the technology boom of 1998—2000, the rules changed. Numerous early-stage telecommunications companies with almost no financial histories sought services from my group at Goldman Sachs. Bankers were suddenly thrust in the new position of evaluating businesses based upon unfamiliar technology distinctions. I struggled to grasp the significance of core technologies and discovered that many colleagues faced similar challenges.

In response, I decided to arrange a seminar that would teach telecom technology concepts. As an analyst, I could not alone receive the attention and support of my group's leaders. Therefore, I coordinated with peers to collectively pitch the proposal. Eventually, management supported the project and suggested that internal industry experts lead a seminar. I surveyed my peers to understand problem areas and developed a syllabus. Goldman's experts repeatedly cancelled the session, however, as they considered training a relatively low priority in the midst of the chaotic deal environment. After researching alternatives, I suggested that we set a firm date and hire external technology consultants to provide a more comprehensive, albeit costly, seminar. Management accepted this proposal and more than two hundred attendees from multiple investment banking groups attended the full day of training. According to colleagues' comments, the firm both targeted clients more carefully and advised them more intelligently as a result.

While selling this expensive alternative to group leaders, I learned the importance of building a coalition and articulating a proposal in appropriate terms. Management

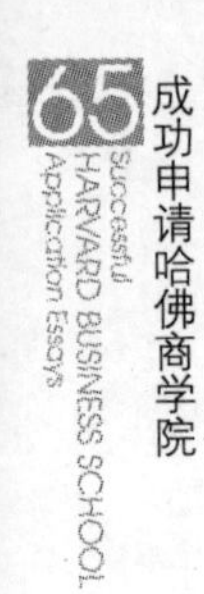

committed funds once I detailed how the training would help the firm win additional business and not serve merely as continuing education. I also learned that identifying a problem is not enough to contribute to an organization. Leadership requires persistence to develop and implement a solution in the face of institutional resistance.

点评

申请人在本文中达成了自己三个重要的目的：第一，他提供了一个自己作为领导者的事例，生动、简洁。这段经历明确展现了他的主动性，以及推进项目直至完成的能力。有关征求支持的细节，增强了他所遇挑战的可信度，以及他所付出的努力程度。

第二，他提出了自己对于“领导力”这个基本概念的理解。光有一个好点子是不够的，一个有效的领导者需要联合多方力量，克服组织的惯性。糟糕的沟通能力可能致命，不够执着或不够坚定也一样。成功的领导者不可能是一名光杆司令。

第三，可能也是最重要的，文中的具体实例与抽象的领导力概念非常贴合，这两部分相互促进，把申请人塑造成了一位富有成效且深思熟虑的商人。

有一点是在写领导力方面的Essay时需要特别注意的，虽细小却很重要。文中，申请人写道：“我协调了各位同事，一起推动这项倡议。”这话含糊不清，有点危险。申请人的努力可以被解读为他参与了这件事情，而不一定是领导者。好在本篇Essay的其余内容清楚地表明了他是主要负责人。所以，你在写Essay时应该尽量避免使用这类模棱两可的措词。

【参考译文】

在传统意义上，投资银行在接受一家公司作为其客户之前，会进行一番详尽的财务审核，以便了解该公司的前景状况，而在1998—2000年的科技大爆炸期间，这套规则改变了。众多处于初创期的通信公司，几乎没有任何财务历史，都来要求我所在的高盛公司团队为他们提供服务。突然之间，银行家们被强行推到一个新位置——基于自己不熟悉的科技领域特性来评估业务。我手忙脚乱地尝试掌握核心科技的意义，发现很多同事也面临着类似的挑战。

为了应对这一挑战，我决定安排一场培训通信科技概念的研讨会。作为一名分析师，仅仅靠我一个人是无法得到团队领导的注意和支持的，因此，我协调了各位同事，一起推动这项倡议。最终，管理层支持开展这个项目，并建议由内部的行业专家来主持这个研讨会。我在同事中间进行了调研，以了解问题所在，然后设计了一份摘要。然而，高盛的专家们一次又一次地取消这场研讨会，因为他们认为，在如此混乱的商业环境中，培训是优先级相对较低的事情。在调研了一些替代方案之后，我建议敲定一个日期，邀请外部科技顾问来主持一场虽昂贵却更全面的研讨会。管理层接受了这项提议，200 多名来自多个投行团队的人员参加了这场全天的培训。据同事们评价，这场培训会之后，公司不仅能更谨慎地挑选目标客户，还能为客户提供更具建设性的建议。

在我向公司领导推荐这个昂贵的替代方案的过程中，我学到了与人联手，以及用恰当的词汇陈述一项建议的重要性。在我详细解释了培训可以如何帮助公司赢得更多生意，而不仅仅是一场继续教育学习之后，管理层就痛快地批了款。我还了解到，要为公司作出贡献，仅仅指出问题所在并不够。在面临制度上的抵制时，领导力还要求领导者坚持不懈地找出解决方案，并贯彻执行。

05
行动的重要性

The market for my firm's software was hot, and engineering was racing to keep up with demand. Quality suffered. We could hand-hold customers through quality problems when we had three customers. Suddenly, we had three hundred.

For nine months, my team had struggled to support our new customers on a promising yet often unreliable product. I knew something needed to change. At the kickoff of our next release, I preached a new approach to our work. We needed to focus on quality, and we needed to make our product easier to use and maintain. The team voiced strong approval for my vision. Nothing changed.

Words alone were not enough. Change would require creativity and deliberate action on my part. I worked to develop procedures to change my group's culture. I built more time into project plans for testing. I implemented new quality measurements to quantify the coverage of our tests. I challenged the team to beat aggressive coverage targets in each project milestone. I added quality as a regular discussion item in weekly meetings and publicly recognized excellent efforts to improve reliability.

With constant reinforcement, the team culture shifted. In short time, the quality assurance department joked that my team was not producing enough bugs. Our chief architect held my project up at a manager's meeting as "an example of how projects at the company should be run." Senior management adopted my team's quality metrics as the standard for measuring quality for each group. Other managers who had originally questioned my plan to invest more engineering time in testing now began to imitate it.

A leader must understand where the company is, where it needs to be, and how the company culture needs to evolve to get it there. Through this experience, I learned that a leader cannot just preach a vision. A leader must initiate action to shape corporate culture and drive change.

点评

本文又是一例成功领导组织内变革的例子。正如前两位一样，本文申请人也指出，好点子本身不足以改变根深蒂固的组织行为。与众不同的是，申请人详细叙述了自己如何从失败中吸取教训。他并不羞于承认当初的“光说不练”缺乏成效，若换作别人处于当时的情境，可能就此偃旗息鼓，而申请人却更加坚定信念，逐步开展具体行动以推动变革。文章把他描绘成一位执着却不失灵活性的工作卓有成效的领导者，同时，这段经历本身也恰到好处地体现了申请人对领导力概念的总结。结尾段写道，领导力需要经常锻炼，而且不能停留在抽象的“愿景”上。这表明，申请人已经从中吸取了宝贵的经验。

【参考译文】

我们公司研发的软件在市场上热卖，工程部不得不加班加点保证供应，产品质量也因此受到了影响。只有三家客户时，我们可以和他们携手解决遇到的问题。但突然间，我们的客户数量达到了300家。

9个月以来，我们的团队一直努力为使用这款有发展前景但性能不稳定的产品的客户提供技术支持。我意识到这种情况必须有所改变。于是在版本升级之际，我提出了新的工作方向：将重点放在保证产品质量上，简化产品的操作和维护。团队内部呼声强烈，对我的建议深表赞同，但情况没有任何改变。

光说不练假把式。要想改变，我需要发挥创造力，谨慎地行动。我制订了一系列改变团队文化的手段。拉长项目的预计时限，用于程序调试；贯彻新的

质量标准，量化程序调试的范围。我要求团队成员在项目进展的每个阶段，积极超越项目的高难度目标。我把产品质量问题作为每周例会的又一项例行讨论话题，公开表扬那些为提高产品的安全性而作出的优异成绩。

经过我反复重申，团队文化有所改变。没过多久，质量保证部门的同事就开玩笑说，我们团队没有生产出足够的“程序故障”。在一次经理会议上，总设计师提出来要把我领导的项目当作“公司项目运行的模范”。高层管理人员采纳我们团队的质量控制标准作为公司所有团队的质量测定标准。有些经理原本对于我拉长制造时间用于调试颇有微词，现在也开始借鉴该方案。

领导者必须清楚公司现状和发展目标，并思考公司文化应该如何顺应公司发展。我从这段经历中学到，领导者不能只是提出愿景而已，必须要发起行动，塑造企业文化，推动变革。

06
危急情况下的领导魄力

USS Georgia hurtled through the Pacific hundreds of feet below the surface, and I was at her helm as Officer of the Deck. Our submarine's massive battery was almost drained, common after a day of intense training, when I received an emergency report that a failed instrument had shut down the reactor. Without an operational reactor or fresh air for the diesel generator, the ship had to rely solely on its nearly depleted battery for electrical power. Unless I took decisive action, *Georgia* would go dead in the water. Consequently, I ordered all non-vital electrical loads switched off and turned my focus to driving our 18,000-ton warship to periscope depth to snorkel on the diesel.

The sonar team reported that they could hear numerous ships, so I conducted several tactical maneuvers to estimate range, course, and speed of each. The results were disconcerting. One ship was close, and it would take skill to avoid hitting it. With the battery quickly discharging though, I dared not wait to reevaluate. I chose a course and ordered the diving officer to bring the ship to periscope depth. As we came shallow, the diesel started, and the battery was unloaded. I peered out the periscope and watched a supertanker pass safely down our side.

As I coordinated the efforts of the crew to "fight the ship," I was invigorated. Performing a successful approach to periscope depth under these intense circumstances was deeply rewarding. Afterward, when I wondered why I felt excited rather than scared or upset, I realized that I thrive on working with a team to accomplish difficult goals and performing well in stressful situations.

点评

申请人用 272 个单词向录取委员会证明了自己完全具备领导者的能力。第一段用简洁的语言展开故事的背景以及其中的困难所在，第二段描述了“将潜水艇上浮”这个决策背后的快速思考过程。毫无疑问，申请人能够在压力下作出艰难的选择，并承受预期的风险。本文最后一段至关重要。肾上腺素飙升的一刻若不能引发事后思考，那它就不过是过眼云烟。这里，申请人显然是个会在事后回顾这类经历的人，并且通过这些经历重新认识自己。

从本文中还可以看出，领导力并不局限于管理团队或引导组织变革，领导力还体现在领导者有权替他人作出关键决策上，这一点是前面几位申请人不曾涉及的。申请人眼见可能要全军覆没，迅速作出艰难决策，最终拯救了他的潜艇以及众船员。他处理压力（甚至是享受压力）的能力证实了他的领导才能。

本文尚有可提高之处。比如，尽管申请人在总结句里提到了团队合作，但他讲的故事不太能看出其他船员在处理这个危机时所扮演的角色。而且，在描述错误决策将导致的严重后果上再多说一两句，能进一步强调他所面临的压力。如果最后能再总结一下领导力——包括当机立断的魄力以及率领团队完成艰难任务的能力，本文将给人更大的冲击力。

【参考译文】

美国海军“乔治娅”号在太平洋水面数十米下疾驰，作为它的航海值日官，我正在舵柄旁值班。潜水艇的巨型电池几乎消耗殆尽，经过一天的密集训练，这种情况很普遍。这时，我接到了一份紧急报告，有个设备出了状况，关闭了反应堆。反应堆不工作，而柴油发电机又没有新鲜空气，整艘潜水艇的用电就全靠这块即将耗尽的电池了，若不当机立断，“乔治娅”号就会沉入水底。于是，我命令关闭所有不重要的用电设备，集中精力将我们这艘 18 000 吨重的军舰升至潜望深度，让柴油发电机换气。

声呐部门报告，他们测到周围有许多船舰，所以我进行了战术策划，评估每艘舰的范围、航线及速度，结果令人不安。有一艘舰靠得很近，需要一些技巧才能避免相撞。然而，电池的电量还在快速下降，我不敢贻误时机再次评估。我选择了一条航线，命令潜水官将潜水艇升至潜望深度。随着我们逐渐靠近水面，柴油发动机开动的同时，电池不再工作。我紧盯着潜望镜，看到一艘“巨型坦克”安全地在我们潜水艇下方驶过。

在协调众船员一起与潜水艇“搏斗”时，我感觉精力充沛。在重重危机下，成功执行升至潜望深度的方案是极有成就感的。后来，我回想自己当时为什么会兴奋，而不是害怕，或者沮丧，我发现，我的成长就在于跟团队成员一起实现艰难的目标，以及在高压状态下出色地完成任务。

07
相信自己，凭直觉行事

In late 1999, I was promoted to marketing director for Ford Turkey. My immediate task was to raise profitable market share in the short-tcrm while improving the brand's image so as to propel sustainable future growth. Given the great freedom the position entailed, I was charged with conceiving and implementing plans to realize our sales targets.

Being effective required that I overcome three distinct challenges.

First, making the transition to marketing director demanded that I gain a firm grasp on all of the department's functions and ongoing projects very quickly. The combination of my analytical skills and ability to focus on multiple tasks simultaneously enabled me to expedite the transition process and become effective in my job almost immediately.

Second, because I was the youngest manager in the company, I had to gain the respect of and build a great rapport with staff. By utilizing my interpersonal skills and establishing weekly departmental meetings and social events, I earned the staff's trust through clearly communicating my vision for the department and providing a forum for their opinions, ideas, and concerns as well as infusing the department with greater "team spirit."

Third, I had to prepare for the imminent launch of two new cars. My strong negotiation skills enabled us to acquire the services of new, better advertising firms at half the previous cost. We also reformulated our brand communication strategy so as to create a unified message that encompassed all our products. The sum of the innovative approaches I led was an increase in overall market share from 5.5 percent to 7.7 percent in fewer than eighteen months and in spite of Turkey's ongoing financial crisis.

Besides confirming my confidence in my leadership skills and motivating my desire to reach a top-level executive position, this experience taught me that the key to success is setting high goals while conveying the belief that they are attainable. Additionally, I learned that managers must trust and act upon their intuition when a situation calls for urgent action.

点评

尽管本文讲述的内容与拯救世界或避免灾难无关，却是展示申请人领导才能的绝妙例证。文章背景是职位升迁，这点对于申请人来说稀松平常。申请人没有强调升职这件事（这算一项成就，可未必证明申请人拥有领导潜能），而是通过指出特定管理难题、描述克服难题动用的技能等展示了他的多才多艺。申请人解释了他如何运用多项技能（分析能力、沟通能力、人际交往能力等）来树立自己的威望，达成销售目标。很明显，团队在整个过程中面临着巨大的障碍，但是在他的带领下，一一得以解决。

结尾的经验教训总结与内省相结合，效果不错。但是本文总结的经验教训与正文似乎有点脱节。如果问题与教训之间的逻辑关系再紧密一些，文章会显得更加完美。

【参考译文】

1999年年底，我被提拔为福特公司土耳其分公司的营销总监。上任后的首项任务是，在短期内提高盈利产品的市场份额，同时提升品牌形象，以推动未来的可持续增长。营销总监这个职位自由发挥空间很大，我要负责拟订销售计划，并加以执行。

要想有效开展工作，我得克服三个方面的难题。

第一，作为新上任的营销总监，我需要迅速了解该部门的所有职能，以及现有项目的进度。我具备的分析技能和同时处理多项任务的能力缩短了职位过渡期，工作效率很快就提高了。

第二，因为我是公司里最年轻的经理，所以我得在员工中建立威信，拉近与员工的关系。我规定每周召开部门会议，分享我对本部门的愿景，为部门注入强大的“团队精神”；组织社交活动，施展我的人际交往技能；搭建了一个论坛，供大家发表意见和建议，倾诉各自的想法和顾虑。最终，我赢得了员工的信任。

第三，我要筹备两场迫在眉睫的新车上市发布会。凭借我出色的谈判技巧，新广告公司同意以之前一半的费用为我们提供更好的服务。为了涵盖所有产品的品牌信息，我们还重新规划了品牌传播战略。我推行的创新方案带来的整体成效是：不到18个月的时间，公司整体市场份额从5.5%上升到7.7%，而当时土耳其正遭受金融危机。

这段经历除了让我对自己的领导能力充满信心，激励我力争上游，谋求要职之外，它还告诉我，成功的关键在于制订高远的目标，同时传达实现目标的信念。此外，我还认识到，管理者在危急时刻必须相信自己，凭直觉行事。

08
主动性比职位更重要

In investment banking, projects are executed in small, hierarchical teams. The analyst, the most junior member of the team, is not expected to be a leader. In my experience, however, taking leadership is a personal choice that is not discouraged by the rigid team structure, as the following recent example will show.

The intense project had only four days left to an important client board meeting as I learned that the associate on my team had just been asked to resign, due to the worsening market conditions. She had been in control of the forthcoming presentation and was my closest supervisor on the team. Sad for my colleague and friend, I also feared the project would suffer greatly, and informed the vice president on the team that we needed reinforcements.

Realizing that I probably had the best understanding of the process after this, I took on a leadership role on the project. I walked the team through the financial model and the presentation draft, explaining the assumptions taken, suggested new analysis to conduct and at one point persuaded the team that a proposed analysis would not add sufficient value to the presentation. I made certain we talked to the relevant people to complete our qualitative analysis, and suggested a way to split the work between us. After the client meeting, the senior team members informed me that they appreciated my leadership in the project, driving both the qualitative and the quantitative analysis forward.

In former leadership experiences I have always held a well-defined, formal leadership position, either, for instance, in the form of being a platoon leader or in the form of being the leader of the student teaching evaluation board. Through this experience and similar situations I have learned that leadership more often than not is something you assume, not something that is handed to you. By taking initiative and being proactive I can lead my project or parts of my projects towards a successful completion.

点评

这篇带有转折性的范文很容易被归入“决定性时刻”命题组下，也可以是一位年轻人学习做领导的事例，但都说到了点子上。申请人面临的状况——经理被辞，他不得不捡起这堆烂摊子，准备一个重要演示等，很多申请人都遇到过，特别是在近几年。让本文脱颖而出的不是对问题的描述，而是申请人从这次经验中学到的东西。具体来说，他特别提到了自己原先接受的领导力概念（组织内一个职责定义明晰的职位），又讲述了投行的经历如何改变了这个概念。他的结论是，主动性比你在组织中担当的职位或角色更重要。申请人把自己勾画成一位关键时刻能够站起来独当一面的人，相信他一定会在哈佛商学院以及今后的事业中茁壮成长。

本文有一点尚待完善，即第一段应该更加直截了当，开门见山。考虑到字数有限，开头一两句话就吸引读者的注意力是很重要的。可以看出，申请人想在开头就设定好故事的背景：他如何在出人意料的情况下担当起领导责任。但随着故事的展开，读者可以明显看出他的境况，因此显得第一段有点多余。Essay 的字数有限，一定要字斟句酌。

【参考译文】

在投资银行内部，一个项目通常由一个等级森严的小团队负责。分析师是团队中资格最浅的成员，没人会期望由他来统领大局。然而，在我的经验中，担当领导责任是个人的选择，并不会被僵化的团队架构所阻拦。下面这个近期发生的事例正展现了这一点。

还剩4天，一个紧迫的项目马上就要在一位重要客户的董事会上演示了，这时我得知，由于市场状况日益恶化，我们团队的经理刚被辞退了。她是我在团队里的直属上司，迫在眉睫的这场演示也是由她负责的。在为我的同事兼朋友哀伤的同时，我也担心这个项目会受到严重影响，于是我向团队的副总裁提出我们需要支援。

我意识到，经理走了之后，我大概是团队中最了解这个项目流程的人了，于是我主动担当起了这个项目的领导职责。我向团队成员详细介绍了该财务模型和演示草稿，并解释其中引用的假设。我还建议进行新的数据分析，说服团队取消其中一项提议的分析，因为其并不能给演示增加多少价值。我确定我们需要与相关人员进行讨论，来完成有质量的数据分析，并提议如何在我们之间划分工作任务。客户的会议结束后，团队的资深成员告诉我，他们非常感激我在这个项目中担起领导责任，推动了定量数据和定性数据分析工作的进展。

在之前的领导经历中，我总是站在一个正式的领导位置上，有着明晰的职责定义，比如排长、学生教学质量评估会的负责人等。通过这次经验以及一些类似的状况，我认识到，领导力通常并不止于你担当的职责，也不止于交托给你的任务。我凭借主动性和前瞻性，让我的项目或部分项目得以成功收尾。

A TYPICAL DAY

命题 2
典型的一天

While recognizing that no day is typical, describe a representative day.

尽管我们知道没有哪一天是典型的一天，不过还是请描述一下你具有代表性的一天。

解题思路

“描述一下你具有代表性的一天”，乍看之下，会觉得这个命题简单至极。不要掉以轻心，这是一个值得花上些时间写的命题，如果写得好，可以充分展现你的个性、处世方式，以及你解决问题的风格。

你的工作时间表和按小时详细记录的日志都不重要，重点是你如何挑选想要表达的内容。简单罗列你所做的事情并不能帮你赢得高分，你的简历大概早就涵盖了你的大部分工作（或者说，应该是这样的），所以这是个机会，让你可以展示自己为什么擅长做这些事情，以及将来作为哈佛商学院的一分子，你可以为这个群体带来怎样的经验。

从我们精选的这几篇经典 Essay 中可以看出，可以使用的写作思路很多。这类命题可以稍稍跳出规则，没有必要按照时间顺序来描写你的一天。不过，很多人的 Essay 写作顺序仍是如此，所以，你若最终照此思路写这个命题，也并非不可。

除了表现种种可行的写作思路外，我们还尽量挑选那些充分表现申请人性格和个性的范文。有几篇文章诙谐幽默，不过大部分不是；有几篇文章结构严谨，同样，也有很多不是。文采斐然可以加分（有时帮助极大），却并非录取的先决条件。先决条件是什么呢？要能表现出你的观点、镇定以及成熟，这些也是我们精选的范文的共同之处。

几乎所有提交申请的申请人都做过一些有趣且重要的事情，所以，简单地罗列或重申你曾做过的有趣且重要的事情是无法将你和众人区别开来的。关键是，不要低估一个看似极为简单的命题。这是一个额外的机会，帮助录取委员会更多地了解你以及你的世界观。

点评人： 丹·埃尔克（Dan Erck）

09
咨询顾问，了解并参与一切

Alarm clock. Clock radio. Cereal. Multivitamin. Rain. No jog today.

The firm represents your career as one pyramid inverted on top of the other. The bottom pyramid represents analysts and associates; the top pyramid, junior and senior partners. At the fulcrum is the case manager. It is the best and worst role at the firm.

Five new voice mails, 12 new e-mails. Scan *Red Herring*, *Venture Wire*, *American Banker*, *WSJ*, and *the NY Times*. Must stay current, I rationalize. Client calls. "Could we have an update before the presentation to review the findings?" The presentation is only four days away. "Absolutely." "I'll see you tomorrow in Parsippany at eight-thirty A.M."

The best part is that you see and do it all. You watch partners agree to outrageous proposals. You design the analysis to execute those proposals. You learn your clients' quirks and earn their confidence. You guide your team. You support the firm, too—writing articles, giving recruiting seminars on "cracking a case interview."

A partner stops by: "I promised Tom that we would incorporate the perspective of Japanese beverage executives." Panic. The analyst reminds you of his vacation. Meet with case team. Reshuffle work plan. Interview client CFO. Rewrite executive summary (again). Gently, have "career concerns" discussion with advisee.

The worst part is that you see and do it all. It is all ultimately your responsibility: the right answer, a happy client, a non-mutinous case team, the partner appearing at the meeting and remembering the topic. You are one part uber-analyst, one part therapist, one part administrative assistant. Secretly, I like this responsibility, too.

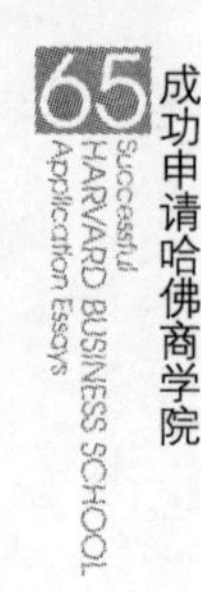

What time does the gym close? Business plan needs another iteration. Girlfriend calls: "We are meeting for dinner at nine, right?" Panic. E-mail document to client. Grab a taxi. Rain. Everything will be fine. It always is.

点评

让一个咨询师陈述此命题，想想就觉得可怕。咨询师的日常工作众人皆知，还要把这一天描写出趣味性从而让自己鹤立鸡群，这绝非易事，可本文的申请人却出色地完成了该任务。

幽默的口吻给文章增添了色彩，申请人对工作的成熟（同时诚实）的观点也非常关键：作为一名项目经理，同时又要满足同事、合伙人、客户以及业余生活对他的诸多要求。文章风格清新，节奏明快。最后一句“一切都会好的，一直都是”触动人心。这句话是在告诉录取委员会，申请人没被日复一日的压力折磨而忽视全局，忘记生命中真正重要的东西。不管你从事什么工作，能够从全局理解自己的工作（即把点连成面）都是宝贵的能力，可以展示出你的稳重和成熟。由本文还可以得到一点启发：300 字就能写出大文章。不用担心自己文笔平平，但一定要花时间思考你的工作是什么，以及为什么能够胜任这份工作？尽量用简短的语言表达，再加上一点点个性特质。

【参考译文】

闹钟。钟控收音机。谷物早餐。复合维生素片。雨天。今日不晨跑。

公司把职业生涯描述成一个倒金字塔叠在另一个金字塔之上。下面的金字塔代表分析师和助理，上面的金字塔代表初级和高级合伙人，而两个金字塔的连接点是项目经理。这是公司里最好的差事，也是最坏的差事。

5 通新留言，12 封未读电子邮件。扫读《红鲱鱼》杂志、《创业投资报》、《美国银行家》、《华尔街日报》和《纽约时报》。要紧跟时代，我试图自圆其说。

客户来电："可否在报告会之前说一下最新进展，看看你们的调查结果？"距离报告会只剩4天时间。"当然可以。""我明天早上8点半在帕西波尼等你。"

最好的角色是，你了解并参与所有一切。你看着合伙人接受那些离谱的提案。你设计分析思路，落实那些提案。你对客户的怪癖了如指掌，他们也信任你。你带领团队。你还要做公司的行政支持：写通讯稿，培训负责招聘的团队"如何搞定案例面试"。

有位合伙人顺道经过："我答应过汤姆，我们会吸收日本饮料行业的管理者观点。"紧张。有位分析师提醒你，他将去休假。与项目团队开会。重新调整工作计划。与客户的首席财务官面谈。（再次）重写执行摘要。与受训学员和婉地探讨"职业困境"。

最坏的角色同样是你了解并参与所有一切。最终，一切责任都将落在你身上：给出最佳方案，带来满意客户，安抚项目队伍，确保合伙人出席会议并记得会议主题。你的一个身份是超级分析师，另一个身份是治疗师，还有一个身份是行政助理人员。告诉你一个秘密，我也喜欢承担这样的责任。

健身房什么时候关门？商业计划需要再次重写。女朋友打来电话："我们9点一起吃晚饭，对吧？"紧张。把文件用电子邮件传给客户。拦下一辆出租车。依然下雨。一切都会好的，一直都是。

10
管理者，忙碌却充满反思

My run ends on Parliament Hill; through mist I pick out a beautiful, distant dome—St. Paul's. Suffocating subway journey crushes the inspiration; people become silent, menacing competitors for space. Humanity revived by brief exchange of funny faces with a bored child.

Immediate interrogation by Francoise, our receptionist, for post-party gossip; we laugh as I promise full disclosure later. Skim through industry newsletters. Alta Vista in trouble; Streetmap, an important partner, moving into mobile. Call friends at both with ideas on working together. 9:30—a session with our marketing and sales directors, on developing a "money channel." I'm skeptical. Can we really improve on existing services? We discuss my concerns about this, its fit with our brand values, and its impact on current finance partners. A fascinating session. Then I probe specifics. What additional work is required? Who will do what, by when?

Back to four voice mails from companies wanting to work with us. Call each back, hoping for that rare gem of an idea; form rapid judgments. Choose one for further analysis in my weekly "new ideas review."

Quick sandwich, then see the MD of BeFree, our affiliate program technology partner. I outline three aims for the 2002 contract. He's baffled when I talk about reducing the burden on Kertreena in our finance team before I mention pricing. Then to concierge services provider TenUK—we're excited about plans to unlock the revenue potential of a Jeeves-branded concierge service—our first wholly "off-line" project.

No meetings after 6:00. I study *the Economist* "mobile internet" survey—an area I'm keen to bring Ask Jeeves closer to. Research some suppliers before I shut down. Reflect on the day. Where should the company be going? Will everything I did today help us get there?

Then a different world. The London debut of Nadia Cole, a young Canadian pianist. Still can't agree with my musical friends on the merits of her Liszt…

点评

这篇文章节奏明快，语言精练。"Alta Vista 公司身陷困境"（Alta Vista in trouble）这一句可以加个动词，其他句子也是。没关系，时间紧迫。工作节奏快，无心考虑这些细枝末节。这就是网络时代的生活。申请人在开头本可以一笔代过，但相反，他选择将一切生活细节描写得富有意义。申请人漂亮地设计了他的一天。第一段就表明了这一点：是的，他很忙，但还没有忙到视圣保罗圆顶这样的美景而不顾；仍然葆有童心，在地铁上与孩子扮鬼脸。结尾尽管略显陈词滥调（互联网创业公司的工作与听一位古典音乐钢琴师的演奏形成对比），不过也强调了在工作之外，申请人还有更丰富的生活。

本文的关键信息出现在文章的后半部分，即申请人介绍完他日常所做所想的各种事情之后。一个结论性的问题（我今天做的每件事会帮助我们实现目标吗？）证明了他在反思：虽然他繁忙地周旋于多个任务之间，但他并不是百分之百地确定他做的每件事情都在帮助公司从 A 成长到 Z——也不确定 Z 就是他们努力的目标。这样的反思是"典型的一天"命题的一个重要且有力的元素。事实上，申请人若多分享一些他的反思，就能给他的文章增加深度。正如本章中的其他范文一样，成熟度加上个人视角的描写比描述一天的日常事务更重要。

【参考译文】

跑步到了议会山。透过薄雾，我一眼瞥见远方那漂亮的圆顶——圣保罗大

教堂。憋闷的地铁之旅令人灵感尽失。人们沉默不语，对胆敢靠近的人怒目而视。跟一位无聊的小孩互扮鬼脸，人性复苏了。

一进门就被前台弗朗索瓦丝逼问派对之后有何花边新闻，我答应稍后向她彻底交代，我们相视大笑。浏览行业新闻，Alta Vista 公司身陷困境；而 Streetmap 公司，一位重要合作伙伴，进军移动业务。致电在这两家公司工作的朋友，商讨合作的主意。早上 9 点 30 分，与市场销售总监开会，讨论开发“资金渠道”。我对此持保留态度：我们真的能提高现有的服务吗？我们进一步讨论了我的疑虑、品牌价值的认同度，以及对我们目前的融资合作伙伴的影响。一场卓有成效的会议。之后，我开始探寻具体细节：还需要做些什么？谁去完成？何时完成？

回来后查看留言，有 4 通来自有合作意向的公司的留言。一一回复，希望能找到一个珍贵的点子，并迅速作出判断。从我的每周“新点子回顾”中挑选其中之一作进一步分析。

吞下三明治，会见联合项目的技术提供方 BeFree 公司的市场总监。我勾画了 2002 年合同的三个目标。在我提到定价之前，我谈到要减轻融资团队科特里娜的工作量，他一脸迷惑。接着会见门房服务提供商 TenUK。我们计划对 Jeeves 品牌的门房服务收费——这是我们第一个“线下”项目，为此十分激动。

下午 6 点之后没有安排会议。研读《经济学人》上的“移动网络”调研——我热切地期望引领 Ask Jeeves 往这个领域发展。关机前，我又调研了几家供应商。回顾这一天的工作：公司的发展方向在哪里？我今天做的每件事会帮助我们实现目标吗？

之后是一个全然不同的世界。纳迪亚·科尔，一位年轻的加拿大钢琴师，在伦敦首演。依然不同意我的乐友对匈牙利钢琴家李斯特的吹捧……

11
非典型工作者的典型一天

Since graduating from college I have played various roles in various places, including a law student in Boston, a schoolteacher in northern Spain, and an investment banker in New York, London, and Frankfurt. Although it would be impossible to collapse these experiences into a single representative day, I can paint my daily experience with broader strokes. Every day I learned something. Every day I met new people. For these reasons, every day was a challenge.

Every day I learned something new. In Frankfurt I took daily German lessons before work. In New York I learned accounting and corporate valuation on the job. In law school I am learning how to analyze judicial decisions and the policies behind them. Despite the diversity of the past few years, every day has comprised a learning experience.

Every day I interacted with new people from diverse backgrounds. In investment banking I worked with management teams from all over the world, including England, Italy, Finland, and Japan. I argued the merits of the matadors with Spaniards at the bullfights in Madrid. I had dinner with the grandfather of my best friend in Germany, who lived under Hitler's troops in Frankfurt and Khrushchev's in East Berlin. Every day was typified by a unique interaction, however small, with someone who widened my perspective on the world.

Due to these elements, every day has been a challenge. Meeting new people, whether they were clients, coworkers, or classmates, has compelled me to try to understand their distinct viewpoints. Adjusting to new cultural and professional environments has consistently challenged me to readjust my outlook, and staggered me with how much I have yet to learn. My representative day has been alternately frustrating and enrapturing. It has been educational, humbling, enthralling, and demanding. But it has never been boring.

点评

这篇短文虽然不合传统，却写得极为精彩。申请人不顾风险，没有描述单独有代表性的一天，而是泛泛地展示他如何对待每一天。像这样的 Essay 写作方式容易弄巧成拙，但这篇范文却完成得非常出色。

申请人在多个城市做过多种工作，他不希望录取委员会把他单纯地看作一个经纪人或者一名律师，而是把他看作一个好奇心十足，喜欢新鲜事物的人。申请人是在告诉录取委员会，他将在哈佛商学院这样一个多姿多彩的地方茁壮成长。丰富的阅历是申请人的竞争优势，同时文章还暗示了他会使课堂讨论更精彩。

申请人认为“每天都是挑战”，为他还有如此多的不知道的事物而“震惊”，这使他显得谦虚且平易近人。这一点至关重要。但凡失败的短文，都是由于基调不正。还有一个重要的启发：陈述此话题也能自由发挥。多数申请人用时间顺序讲述他们典型的一天，但是正如此范文展示的，其他形式也同样有效。

【参考译文】

大学毕业后，我游历各国，从事过各色工种。在波士顿读法律学校，在西班牙北部当小学教师，在纽约、伦敦、法兰克福做投资银行家。尽管要从这些经历中提炼出典型的一天是不可能的，但是我可以粗略描述一下我的日常经历。每天，我都能学到新东西。每天，我都能结识新朋友。因此，每天都是挑战。

每天都学到新东西。在法兰克福的那段日子里，每天上班前我要学德语。到了纽约，我又在工作中学习会计知识和企业评估。进了法学院，我又开始学习分析司法裁决及其判决依据。尽管过去几年的经历纷乱无序，但每一天都是一段新的学习经历。

每天与不同背景的人打交道。在投资银行工作时，共事的管理团队成员来自五湖四海，有英国人、意大利人、芬兰人和日本人等。在马德里斗牛场，我会跟西班牙人争论各个斗牛士的优点。在德国，与我最好的朋友的祖父共进晚餐。老人曾生活在希特勒军队统治下的法兰克福，后迁往赫鲁晓夫统治的东柏林。每天与别人的交流无论多么简短，都会拓宽我的视野，成为典型的一天。

因此，每天都是挑战。与不同的人接触时，不管对方是客户、同事还是同学，我都会努力理解他人的观点。为了适应新的文化氛围和工作环境，我不得不时时重新调整自己的人生观，也为自己还有如此多的不知道的事物而震惊。我的典型的一天总是悲喜交加，既引人深思，又令人谦卑；既引人入胜，又压力重重。但是，绝不会令人乏味。

12
分析师，积极专注于工作

Early morning. A genomics laboratory in Germany.

I drop reagent into vials containing my skin cell scrapings and the chief scientific officer nods approval. Due diligence is always engaging, but it rarely provides the opportunity to purify one's DNA. I had asked to experiment with the company's new testing kits in order to evaluate whether the technology is simple enough to permit layperson use, as management touts. This analysis will support my investment case.

I next meet with the company's CEO. We trade fresh biotech gossip and then I challenge the growth rates he is projecting for a new business unit, citing evidence from my own industry analysis. In the past few years I have learned to balance a strong company rapport with the ability to ask tough questions. En route to the airport, I call Fidelity portfolio managers with my revised thesis and downgraded numbers on this company and urge them to sell their stock. As the sole European biotechnology analyst, the portfolio managers rely on my guidance to position their funds.

Back in the London office.

I write a note of thanks in Italian to a company that visited our office the previous week. My U.S. counterpart calls. I had suggested that we share industry insights on a regular basis to help each other pick stocks. Now we are working together to determine whether a recent spate of profit warnings from the life science companies are isolated events or indicative of a slowdown in capital equipment spending.

Prowling the corridors, later that day.

Armed with DCF spreadsheets and Play-Doh, I talk through pipeline assumptions with a dubious fund manager. I construct model antibodies and drug receptors to explain how a Nordic company I want him to buy makes drugs with superior side effects. He calls trading to build a position, and I am pleased with the results of my interactive teaching.

Evening, markets closed. Stocks at rest. I wonder what intrigue they will bring tomorrow. I head home to stir-fry a dinner for friends with my new wok.

点评

本篇 Essay 是一篇好范文，呈现了一位既务实又存有好奇心的分析师形象。申请人强调他不仅会分析数据，而且会向 CEO 提刁钻的问题，然后回到办公室给基金经理解释复杂的科技。他专注于自己的工作，又不至于太投入而丢失了评价公司所必需的视角。正是这种成熟让申请人从每年数百名申请哈佛商学院的证券分析师中脱颖而出。申请人不是简单地交代“这就是我的工作”，而是将它带上了一个层面——展示他为什么认为他比其他类似背景的申请人更出色。

本篇 Essay 语调自信，但不居高临下。申请人是在告诉哈佛商学院：“这就是为什么我对自己的事业如此在行——选择我吧！”你可以看出申请人对他的所作所为很自豪，而且相信自己为同事们提供帮助。这里值得注意的一点是，不要羞于展示你擅长做自己所从事的工作。然而，注意你的表达方式。不要骄傲自大，要谦恭温和地证明你为什么擅长自己的工作，为什么你的日常工作在广义上来说是相关联的。

【参考译文】

一大早，德国基因组学实验室。

我将试剂滴进装有我的表皮碎屑的小瓶里，首席科学官点头同意。像这样的调查总是充满吸引力，不过很少有机会能像这次实验一样，提炼一个人的DNA。为了评估这项科技是否像管理层所兜售的那样——操作简易，外行人能轻松上手，我要求试用公司这组新测试套装。其分析数据将支持我的投资项目。

接着，我会见了公司CEO。我们闲谈了几句生物科技领域的最新八卦，接着针对他预测的新部门增长率提出了质疑，而证据就是我们自己的行业分析数据。过去几年来，我学会了如何在与公司同事和睦共处的同时，又能够抛出刁钻的问题。去机场的路上，我致电富达国际投资公司的投资组合经理，以我修改后的观点以及该公司的降级数据敦促他们抛售股票。作为全欧洲唯一一位生物技术分析师，投资组合经理们依靠我的指导来管理资金。

回到伦敦办公室。

我用意大利文写了一份感谢卡，向一家上周曾造访我们办公室的公司表达谢意。美国的同事打来电话。我曾提议，我们定期交换行业洞见，以帮助彼此挑选股票。现在，我们齐心协力，想要判断近期一系列生命科学企业的利润预警是孤立事件，还是预示着资本设备支出放缓。

下班前，走廊踱步。

我一手拿着现金流量贴现表格，一手拿着橡皮泥，跟一位半信半疑的基金经理解释销售渠道假设。我想让他买进北欧一家公司的股票，于是我构建了抗体和药物受体的模型，用以解释这家公司如何生产轻微副作用的药物。他用电话交易建了仓位。我对这个互动教学的结果很满意。

入夜，股市收盘。股票们休息了。我想象着明天又会有什么策划。回家，用我的新锅为朋友们炒俩菜。

13
亚洲主管，跨越语言和文化障碍

In charge of logistic developments for five Asian factories, I manage project teams for systems implementation and coordinate with local operational teams to make supply chain improvements. I also manage the overall logistics activity of the strategic products manufactured in Asia. These different functions provide an interesting combination of diverse short-term and midterm issues that make no day typical. And today was a representative day.

I started with a phone call to the managers of projects in China and the Philippines. Through these daily reviews I assist them in their difficulties, and we define corrective actions that are followed up the next day.

Mornings are usually kept for operational issues that need to be tackled during the day with Asian teams. Today while shaking hands with the logistics staff of the Bangkok factory, a fault in the invoicing system was reported to me, and I helped to analyze the cause. Later along with the quality department I examined a customer complaint and decided to freeze shipments of a product to check the stock quality.

Lunch was an opportunity to brainstorm with Thailand's production manager on the potential flexibility of a new machine. We planned a meeting to detail the stock savings expected.

Because of the time difference, I usually dedicate afternoons to midterm issues for which I have strong interactions with the French headquarters. Today I consulted with marketing regarding the decision to cease production of a product made in Thailand. Then after a review with the industrial strategy department, I finalized a machine

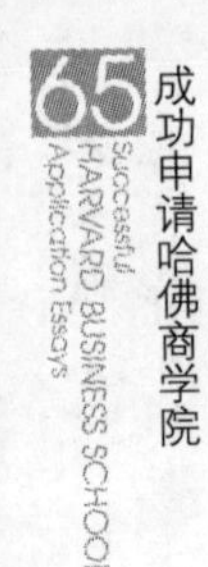

investment midterm plan for the Philippines, in preparation for a business trip there.

My evenings are also active, with dense social life. Today I took a colleague to the opening of my Chinese friend's painting exhibition.

点评

读完本文你一定会认为，申请人每天不停地解决问题、做决策，跨越时区和国家。他诚实地告诉读者，自己肩上扛的责任如此重大，没添加一丝虚言。短文把他描绘成灵活的管理者，必要时能够当场拍板，但若是事情的影响深远，也愿请教他人。申请人看上去是一位能够跨越语言和文化障碍合作沟通的人，是一位成熟稳重、经验丰富而受人尊重的经理。所有这些优势使他成为哈佛商学院有力的候选人，是能够使学校更加丰富多彩的宝贵人才。

如果非要指出需要改进的地方，那就是本文的结尾有待提高。最后提到的社交生活以及对艺术的兴趣如蜻蜓点水，缺乏实质内容。如果再添加一些生活细节，即使无关工作，也可以让读者进一步了解申请人的性格。

【参考译文】

作为5家亚洲工厂后勤工作的主管，我负责管理项目小组进行后勤系统实施，与当地业务小组协调以改善供应链。同时，我还管理着亚洲制造的战略产品的整体后勤工作。不同的职能要求我处理形形色色的中短期事务，使我的每一天都是特别的一天。今天就是典型的一天。

一上班，我先与驻中国和菲律宾的项目经理通电话。通过这样的每日汇报，我协助他们解决困难，次日再一起制订后续修正措施。

通常，与亚洲团队一起工作期间，我会在早上解决亚洲小组需要当天处理的业务问题。今天，曼谷工厂的后勤工作人员刚与我见面，就告诉我开票系统出了故障。于是，我帮助他们分析故障原因。随后，又同质量控制部门一起处理一桩客户投诉，并决定暂停产品出货，清查库存质量。

午餐时，与泰国的生产经理进行头脑风暴，讨论一台新机器的潜在适应性。又安排了一次会议，详细讨论期待解决的库存节省问题。

由于时差的关系，我通常在下午处理中期问题，即那些需要与法国总部进行多次沟通的问题。今天，我向市场部门咨询是否停产一款泰国制造的产品。与工业战略部门讨论之后，最终确定了菲律宾工厂增设机器的中期计划，并准备前往那里出差。

夜生活依旧充实，社交活动频繁。今天，我要带同事去参加一位中国朋友的画展开幕式。

14
银行家，高压节奏下寻找平衡生活

A Day in the Life

7：30 A.M.： Alarm clock blares with the Beatles: "Wake up. Get out of bed. Drag a comb across my head. Catch the bus in seconds flat." Perform said lyrics.

8 A.M.： Catch train, skim the headlines of the *WSJ* and then delve into the international section. Get so absorbed almost miss my stop.

9 A.M.-12 P.M.： Review cash flow and valuation analyses prepared by members of the Latin American team. Work with team to confirm growth assumptions and discuss sensitivity of investor returns to currency assumptions.

1 P.M.： Call investment bankers or officers of an investment target and ask questions about inconsistencies or confusing aspects of the financial models they provided. Ask for updates on previously requested questions or documents.

2 P.M.： For a different deal, field a curve ball thrown by the target company's lawyers. Work with these lawyers and our counsel to analyze and discuss the effects of proposed changes in the legal and tax structure of the transaction.

3 P.M.： Call CEO and CFO of target company to tell them what progress we have made and what we still need from their bankers or management team. Brainstorm with them on solutions to comments made by the lawyers. Outline steps for the next few days.

4 P.M.： Meet with my supervisor and the Latin American team. Update them on

my progress and highlight any key outstanding issues or pressure points that must be resolved.

4：30 P.M.： Begin gathering and processing information that will be presented to our investment committee in a few weeks.

6：30 P.M.： Plan goals that need to be accomplished for tomorrow's ten-day trip to Mexico and Brazil.

7 P.M.： Start home. Read.

8 P.M.： Run five miles, watching sunset along the Hudson River.

9：30 P.M.： Meet friends for dinner, jazz show or a movie.

点评

本篇 Essay 直截了当，内容充实。它不打算用超人般的战绩震慑你，而是将申请人塑造成一位努力的员工，尽管身处一个高压、快节奏的行业里，仍然能维持适当、平衡的生活。文中最精彩的一句就是第一段中披头士的歌词，它让你感觉申请人很可能是一个不错的小伙子。这个开场很漂亮（也很好玩），为整篇文章定下了轻松的基调。接下去的一切，是对银行家一天生活的相当规范的描述。然而，申请人前前后后一直都在吸纳拉美团队的意见、参考国际事件的影响，这使他从其他投行同僚中略略胜出。

尽管总体来看，本文出色地完成了命题任务，但申请人可以写得更有深度。引入更有力的事例，如担任领导团队的角色；或者多增加一些回顾反思的内容，都可以使一天的生活更丰富。不过，你无须六七篇作文篇篇都打出本垒打以获得好印象。事实上，无中生有地硬挤出六七篇征服世界的文章，还不如简明、实事求是地回答命题。本文的申请人正是这么做的，而且他获得了成功。

【参考译文】

生命中的一天

7：30：闹钟响起披头士的歌声："醒来，起床，拿起梳子梳头发，数秒冲上巴士车。"

8：30：坐上火车，翻阅《华盛顿日报》的头条新闻，然后专心研读国际版。由于过于投入，差点坐过站。

9：00 到 12：00：重新审视现金流向以及拉美团队准备的估值分析。与团队成员一起确认增长假设，讨论投资者回报率对货币假设的敏感性。

13：00：打电话给投资银行家或投资目标的官员，询问他们提供的融资模型中不一致或含混的内容，要求更新原先询问的问题和文件。

14：00：在另一宗生意上，处理目标公司的律师杀来的回马枪。与这些律师及我方律师一起，分析讨论他们提出的变更对这宗生意的法律和税务结构造成的影响。

15：00：打电话给目标公司的 CEO 和 CFO，通知他们我们已经完成了哪些步骤，还需要他们的银行家或管理层给予什么支持。针对律师们的意见，与他们一起头脑风暴，讨论对策。列出未来几天的行动步骤。

16：00：会见上司及拉美团队。汇报我的工作进展，重点讨论一些亟待解决的关键问题或压力。

16：30：开始收集并处理那些将于数周之后提交给投资委员会的信息。

18：30：明天将前往墨西哥和巴西出差，制订此次出差目标。

19：00：回家。看书。

20：00：跑 8 千米，沿着哈得孙河观赏日落。

21：30：与朋友共进晚餐，听爵士音乐会，或看一场电影。

DEFINING MOMENT

命题3

决定性时刻

We all experience "defining moments;" significant events that can have a major impact on our lives. Briefly describe such an event and how it has affected you.

我们都经历过诸多“决定性时刻”，即对我们的生活产生深远影响的重大事件。简要描述其中一个事件，并说明它如何改变了你的生活。

解题思路

动笔之前，你应该多花点时间，思考一下该命题考察的到底是什么。许多申请人经常会把决定性的事情错当成英雄事迹或崇高事业，希望能讲述与此相应的决定性时刻。别上这个当。不要试图说服录取委员会你的决定性时刻比别人伟大得多，只需简单说明那一刻或那段经历对你的个人发展产生了怎样的影响。

有些决定性时刻确实是英雄式的（例如战胜残疾），如果你有这样的时刻和我们分享，很棒！不过，在叙述时务必要保持谦虚的态度。另一方面，如果你要描述的经历看上去平淡无奇，也不用担心，那个时刻与你从中学到的经验相比，简直无足轻重。

这是一个展示你过往经历的机会。勇敢一点，风趣一点，同时保持自省的态度。可能的话，尽可能多地展示此类经历，但一定要如实描述。你应该避免什么呢？那就是害羞。畏首畏尾通常写不出好文章，无法传达你身上引人注目的品质。记住，抓住这个机会，展示自己！

点评人： 瓦莱丽·瓦尔茨（Valerie Valtz）

15
出租车上的一瞥

Earlier this year, I returned to the place I once left as a child: Asia. During my six-month transfer to Bain & Company's offices in the region, I traveled through some of the world's most impressive airports and tallest skyscrapers. I also witnessed firsthand the poverty that plagued neighborhoods across Asia, from the countryside of Vietnam to street corners near my grandmother's home in Manila. Once, on a trip to Jakarta, my taxi was caught in traffic. As I looked out from my window, I saw a boy, no more than five years old, slowly strolling through lanes on the highway with bags of peanuts. He knocked on every window along the way trying to make a sale, but was ignored by passengers sitting comfortably inside Mercedes sedans chatting on cellular phones.

The prevalent and pedestrian nature of this scene made it a "defining moment" for me. In fact, the lessons from my transfer have inspired my long-term goal to close the widening gap between Asia's elite and its poor. During an e-commerce strategy project for a software client in greater China, I saw a vibrant, entrepreneurial community eager to discover how the new economy will redefine Asia. I am convinced that technology will bring unprecedented opportunities for those enchained by the status quo to lift themselves up. I also experienced the intricacies in dealings with government bureaucracy in my work with a British consumer-product client frustrated with its state-owned monopoly partner in Vietnam. I hope to apply my private sector experience to help development agencies such as the Asia Development Bank confront similar challenges and reach those truly in need.

As Asia continues to bridge its economic divide, the future depends on a new

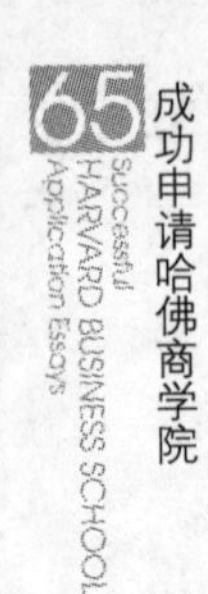

generation of business leaders who embrace innovation and understand how to bring about transformation to a region at the crossroads of change. I am committed to be a part of this *next big wave*.

点评

申请人的决定性时刻在某些方面并不起眼。堵车把他困在出租车的后座上，而唯一有点与众不同的，是事情发生在充满异国风情的雅加达。数星期以来，申请人在一幢幢办公大楼间穿行，飞遍了整个亚洲，而出租车窗外，一个小男孩却为了赚几分钱在卖花生。这一幕令人心酸，在东南亚却随处可见。申请人由此想到，他应该为改善这样的生存环境出一份力。他决定将自己的职业生涯奉献给那些需要帮助的人们。这是一个崇高的目标，而且申请人矢志不渝。这是篇好范文，表明一次普通的经历（坐出租车遇上堵车）同样可以成就伟大的事业。记住，从过往事件中学到的经验教训才是重点，而非经历本身。

虽然结尾成功地从亚洲之旅过渡到当下，但是得出的结论略显开放。申请人给出了实例，说明决定性时刻给他造成了怎样的影响，之后又把我们拉回到万丈高空，含糊地谈到说要做“下一波浪潮”的弄潮儿。如果结尾能够更加明确，整篇短文会更具有说服力。

【参考译文】

今年年初，我回到了童年时代曾经离开的地方：亚洲。在调往贝恩公司亚洲办事处任职 6 个月的时间里，我亲眼见识了全世界最受人瞩目的机场和最高的摩天大楼；也亲眼目睹了亚洲一些穷困潦倒的地区——从越南农村到菲律宾首都马尼拉我祖母家的街头。有一次，在前往雅加达的途中，我乘坐的出租车遇上了堵车。从车窗往外望，我看见一个不超过 5 岁的男孩，正手捧着几袋花生，小心翼翼地穿行于车道之间。他沿途一辆一辆地敲车窗门叫卖花生，但是乘客们舒舒服服地坐在奔驰轿车里打手机，对他不理不睬。

类似的场景处处可见、平淡无奇，但它却成了我的“决定性时刻”。事实上，此次职位调动激励我订下了长远目标，即缩短亚洲日渐扩大的贫富差距。在为中国的一家软件公司制订电子商务战略的项目中，我看到了一个充满活力和创业精神的社会正在重新定位，积极寻求亚洲的新经济。我相信，技术将给那些被现状所困的人们带来前所未有的机遇，提高他们的社会地位。有家英国消费品公司被它的合作伙伴—— 一家越南的国有垄断企业搞得灰头土脸。我在为他们提供咨询服务时，也感受到一股与官僚政府打交道的那种隐晦。我想用我在私有企业中学到的经验，帮助如亚洲开发银行这样的发展机构处理类似的问题，从而让真正有需要的人从中受益。

随着亚洲的经济差距不断缩小，亚洲的未来要依靠新一代的商业领袖。他们追求创新，懂得如何在改革的十字路口实现地区经济转型。我决心要做下一波浪潮的弄潮儿。

16
领导者的孤独

In the summer of 1995, I was selected to serve as an exchange officer with the British Royal Navy. Thus far, my experiences in the U.S. Navy had been interesting, exciting, and amazingly fun: flying in helicopters, firing machine guns, diving to twelve thousand feet in a submarine, etc. I was now assigned to a British destroyer in the North Atlantic, participating in the most intensive assessment program known to the Royal Navy. It included onboard facilitators simulating the most realistic, warlike conditions.

When "war" broke out, explosions went off, power went out, passageways filled with smoke, and casualties lay screaming. I was a firefighter on the damage control team, dispatched to fight a fire in the engine room. I watched three of my men leap down a hatch, and then heard a facilitator yell, "In ten seconds, that fire will spread to the entire ship! What are you going to do?" After a gut-wrenching pause, I ran to the hatch, closed it, and tightened it down.

I forced myself to remember that this was only a drill. It was a defining moment. I had just made a decision that cost the lives of three men. In reality, would I have been able to justify my actions, knowing I had done the right thing and served the greater good? Could I have looked the families of those men in the eye and told them that I had no choice? This event illustrated to me that the greatest challenge of leadership is making impossibly tough decisions when a decision must be made. I learned that after all the soul-searching, you must stand by your decision and move on. I also now see what is meant when people refer to the loneliness of command, the loneliness of leadership.

点评

当爆炸声停止，伤亡人员被抬走之后，浮现在我们面前的是一位年轻的官员，在一次演习中学到了现实世界中宝贵的一课：领导的难处。通过描述一位领导者所遇到的挑战，申请人清楚地展现了自己具备的领导能力，以及令人印象深刻的成熟度。申请人花时间深思由一次经历学到的经验教训（这里的经验教训是，领导者并不总像人们吹嘘的那样风光），是一个很好的榜样。当你在写 Essay 时，你应该花点时间思考，不仅要写出顺理成章的经验教训，还要有你预期之外的东西。

无论你从决定性时刻汲取了怎样的经验教训，都要尽量说明它在之后如何影响了你的生活，本文欠缺的正是这一点——尽管申请人突出了他对领导力的深刻理解，但他没有提及任何有关这段经历如何影响了他今后的选择或决定的事情。

【参考译文】

1995 年夏天，我被选作交换军官，去英国皇家海军服役。到目前为止，我在美国海军的经历一直相当有趣，令人激动、充满惊喜：开直升机，开机关枪，坐潜艇潜到近 4 000 米的海底，等等。现在，我被指派去北大西洋的一艘英国驱逐舰上，参与一项被认为是皇家海军强度最高的演习计划。驱逐舰上安排了位指挥军官，负责模拟最逼真、最接近实战情形的演习。

“战争”爆发后，爆炸声响起，电力被切断，走道里烟雾缭绕，伤兵躺地惨叫。我是抢险队的消防员，被分派去熄灭轮机舱的大火。我看见三位队友跳进了舱内，而这时，指挥军官却大喊道：“还有 10 秒，大火将蔓延全舰！你打算怎么办？”一瞬间，我愣住了，在经历了一番撕心裂肺的挣扎后，我跑向轮机舱口，关上舱门，紧紧地扣下。

我强迫自己记住这只是一场演习。这是一个决定性时刻。我刚刚做了一个决定，而三条人命就因为这个决定而牺牲了。在现实中，即使知道自己做得没错，符合更大的利益，但我能为自己的行为找到正当的理由吗？我能够直视这三位受难士兵的家属，告诉他们我别无选择吗？这个事件告诉我，领导者最大的挑战，是在难以抉择的情境下作出抉择。在我进行了全面的自我反省之后，我认识到，一个领导者必须坚守自己的决定，并继续前进。我也明白了，所谓的“指挥官的孤独”、“领导者的孤独”到底是什么意思。

17
家族生意与心爱事业的两难选择

Upon graduating from college, everyone expected me to join my father's business because I had been working for him part-time since the age of twelve. However, a year before graduation, the firm started experiencing financial difficulties that could have led to bankruptcy. By living through my father's agony to save his business, I experienced firsthand the difficulties and uncertainties involved in his line of work. In addition, the bleak outlook for most small businesses made my future seem even more uncertain had I decided to enter this field.

I faced a dilemma: whether to join the family business or pursue my passion for finance, which was my field of study and a promising sector in Greece at the time. To everyone's surprise, I decided to seek employment in the financial sector. After numerous interviews and several offers, I followed my mentor's advice (my professor Lila Mordochae) and one week after graduating from college I was hired as a financial analyst at Telesis Investment Bank.

In retrospect, the crisis in my father's business has had a lasting impact on my life. This experience taught me to think and plan strategically, with the security and well-being of my family in mind. Experiencing the effects of this crisis, I recognized the significance of thoroughly evaluating the repercussions of my decisions on others prior to any action. In addition, I learned the value of being united with others at all times—family, friends or colleagues— especially during difficult times.

I also realized the significance of being financially independent and of assuming full responsibility for my future. Even though my parents had instilled in me the importance of saving money for a rainy day, it was through this experience that I realized how important it is to do so. I have learned to lead a balanced life: living within my means, enjoying the fruits of my labor, but also saving for future and unexpected needs.

点评

申请人用不加入父亲公司的决定，解释了他如何评判生活、事业的轻重缓急。眼看父亲的公司在破产的边缘飘摇却决定袖手旁观，这是一个非常困难的决定，也是一个不讨人喜欢的决定，但同时，还是一个令人鼓舞的决定。因为从长期来看，申请人的决定是正确的。

在作出职业决定的同时，短文成功地向读者勾画了申请人学到的重要经验。如果能够阐述思考过程中的细节，那么文章将会更有说服力。尽管如此，作为读者，你仍会在读完文章后清楚地感觉到，申请人是一个非常清楚自己想要什么生活的人。

在撰写个人陈述时，要记住一点：提出观点，并且明确表达。与其讲一个动人的故事，不如传达你的信仰或者表现你的为人，更关键的是表达重点。

【参考译文】

大学即将毕业，大家都认为我会加入父亲的公司，因为打从12岁起，我就一直在那儿做兼职。然而，就在毕业前一年，公司开始出现财务危机，几近破产。父亲为了挽救公司痛苦不堪。虽然我熬过了这段阴影，但也从中切身感受到了那一行的艰辛和不稳定。此外，这行里的多数小企业前景黯淡，假如我决意进入这行，未来注定不容乐观。

我面临着两难选择：加入家族生意，还是追求我的金融梦？后者是我的专业，而且当时希腊的金融业前景一片光明。出乎众人的意料，我决定在金融公司谋职。参加了无数场面试后，我收到了几封录用信。遵从导师（莉拉·莫多克教授）的建议，大学毕业一周后，我就进入了特莱西斯投资银行，当上了一名金融分析师。

回顾过去，父亲经历的事业危机对我的生活产生了长远的影响。这件事教会我周全地筹划未来，兼顾家庭的幸福、平安。经历了这场危机，我认识到在行动之前全面评估每项决策对他人产生影响的重要性。此外，我学会了在任何时候都要团结他人——家人，朋友或同事，尤其是在困难时期。

我还意识到经济独立的重要意义，以及为自己的未来全权承担责任的意义。尽管父母早就向我灌输要未雨绸缪，但经过此番事件，我才明白这有多重要。我学会了如何平衡我的生活：自己打拼，尽情享受自己的劳动成果，同时节约用钱，以备不时之需。

18
一次户外经历改变了我的一生

I didn't know what to believe, and with hypothermia setting in, I didn't know if I could make it. The water was 48°F and I had been in it for thirty minutes. Luckily, I was headed back to shore, but it had been a frustrating experience. I had always been a good swimmer and I could have made it back before now, but those weren't the rules. The twelve of us were instructed to swim and finish as a team. Then again, the same people told us the water would be warm and to jump in without wetsuits. After another twenty minutes and constant encouragement, we finally made it. My feeling of pride and newfound confidence showed me just how much I had needed the challenge.

Eagle Lake Wilderness Camp in the Colorado Rockies provided fourteen days of cold, hunger, and exhaustion, which turned into a lifetime of opportunities. Growing up, I was smart and perceptive, but also reserved. I needed to break that paradigm. I needed confidence in my ability to handle stressful, unpredictable situations so that I could develop my potential as a leader.

Our swim was only one of ten challenges faced by our team. I learned much more than how to survive hypothermia, navigate a free rappel, live off the wilderness, and complete a high-altitude half-marathon. I revealed some of my natural leadership qualities like self-understanding and sustained motivation. I demonstrated how to work effectively within teams. I acquired the confidence to pursue leadership responsibilities. I found the will to pursue difficult and exhausting goals along with the stamina to accomplish them. And I learned how to be most effective by encouraging and developing others.

Our team mantra, "This wasn't in the brochure," has since reflected the excitement and challenge of my life. Without the lessons and confidence gained from this experience, I would never have had the ability to run student governments, organize community initiatives or lead consulting project teams.

点评

"一次户外经历改变了我的一生"，这样的故事最怕落入俗套，但本篇 Essay 显然没有，这还多亏申请人出色的讲故事的能力。申请人参加这次训练时只是一个害羞的小男孩，没什么自信，但在经历了体温下降、半程马拉松、蹦极之后，成长为一个有勇气、有信心的人。这个转变实在惊人，申请人证明了自己是一个乐于尝新的人。申请人详细地描述了他是如何改变的，他从这段经历中学到了什么，干得非常漂亮！当你在写 Essay 时，如果你担心你的话题可能不够原创，那就讲一个有说服力的故事，多些精彩的细节。故事写得越具体，你的 Essay 就越成功。

在结尾段落，申请人提到他参加学生会、社区工作，以及在工作中担任领导的经历，这些都是展示"决定性时刻"对他的影响的极好的例子。考虑到字数有限，本文已经没有多余的篇幅用来讨论它们，然而，这些可以成为其他几篇 Essay 的很好的备选主题。如果运用恰当，这些共同的主题可以变成一整组相互连贯、相互呼应的申请文章。

【参考译文】

我的信心动摇了。随着体温下降，我不知道我还能不能游回岸上。水温只有 8℃，而我已经在这样的水里泡了半个小时了。好在我已经开始朝岸上游了，但整个过程真令人灰心。一直以来，我都是个游泳好手。若在平时，这会儿我都站在岸上了。不过，这次我却失败了。这一次，我们 12 个人被要求作为一个团队游完全程。而且，我们还被告知说水温不会太凉，不用穿防寒泳衣。就这样，又过了 20 分钟，在不停地鼓励下，我们终于上岸了。自豪感以及新增的自信表明，我是多么需要这次挑战。

本次位于科罗拉多州落基山脉的鹰湖野外营地提供了为期 14 天的有关饥饿、寒冷、疲劳的极限挑战，这往往是一生中难得的机会。从小到大，我都是一个聪明的、有见解的人，但也很内向。我需要打破这种模式。我需要自信地应对变幻莫测的高压环境，从而发展我的领导潜力。

而游泳只是我们团队接受的 10 个挑战中的一个。我学到的东西，远远多过于如何对抗体温下降、如何成功完成蹦极、如何在野外生存，以及跑完高地半程马拉松等体能方面的锻炼经验。我身上一些与生俱来的领导素质被挖掘出来，比如自我理解、持之以恒。我展示了如何使团队有效合作；收获了承担领导职责的自信心。我发现自己有毅力及精力去完成困难的挑战，并且学会了如何通过鼓励和培养他人，发挥出团队最高的效率。

我们团队的口号——“手册上找不到”，预示了我今后的活力和挑战。若不是在这段经历中得到的经验教训和自信，我绝对不会有能力管理学生会、组织社区活动，或领导项目咨询团队。

19
战胜残疾，学会走路

The most defining moment that I have experienced is overcoming my handicap by learning to walk.

At the age of one, I had to undergo surgery to my spine due to a nonmalignant tumor. The tumor was removed successfully, but during the surgery my nerves were damaged, which resulted in paraplegia. Several doctors told my parents that I would never be able to walk and I was placed in a school for the handicapped.

I was a happy child and at school I ranked the highest in class. As I was growing up, however, I came to have a number of exciting friends, who were able to walk. This made it harder for me to be limited in my own movement. Fortunately, it stimulated my mother to approach a well-known surgeon, who made it possible for me to walk with braces on my legs. After three years I became restless again and I longed to go to a normal school. I was the first in the special school's history to "escape." But my most challenging accomplishment was yet to come. I refused to have any doctor draw my boundaries and I pushed myself through several more operations and an intense period of physical therapy. The impossible came true, as I became able to walk with crutches.

Any handicap will generate a significant amount of emotional turmoil in a person's life. Although I still walk with the help of crutches, my disability hasn't created any barriers in my life that I could not resolve. The contrary happened, as conquering my handicap offered me a sense of achievement and self-confidence that enables me to confront the challenges of life audaciously and with a positive mind. Achieving an accomplishment that I could initially only dream of had a huge influence on my personality.

点评

从开篇第一句话开始，申请人以平铺直叙的语气讲述了他战胜残疾的过程。文章触动了读者的内心，但并不是在乞求怜悯、同情。相反，申请人是一个感激自己所拥有的，并且渴望拥抱生命的人。

毫无疑问，本文讲述的是“英雄事迹”。不过，短文最耀眼的部分是申请人的语调。这是一种温暖人心、如沐春风的语调，给人鼓舞却不居高临下。尽管第一次拄着拐杖走路本身就是感人的一刻，但是最能引起读者共鸣的，是申请人的为人。本篇 Essay 带来的启示是：无论讲述的是英雄事迹还是平凡琐事，这都不要紧，重要的是要让自己看上去是一个值得交往的人。

【参考译文】

我一生中最重要的事情是战胜残疾，学会走路。

一岁那年，我的脊椎上长了良性肿瘤，必须接受手术。虽然医生成功地摘除了肿瘤，但是由于手术中神经受损，我落下了残疾。好几位医生都说，我这辈子不可能走路了。于是，我被送入了一所残疾人学校。

我是个个性开朗的孩子，学习成绩在班里名列前茅。随着我一天天长大，我认识了许多有趣的朋友，他们都会走路，而自己行动不便的事实深深地刺痛了我。幸亏我母亲于心不忍，去找了一位著名的外科医生。他给我的腿装上支架之后，我终于可以走路了。三年后，我的心又开始不安分了。我渴望上正常的学校，我成了这所特殊学校历史上第一个“出逃”的人。但是，最艰巨的挑战尚未到来。我不愿接受任何医生强加给我的“未来”，我逼着自己又做了几次手术，还安排了一段时间的高强度理疗。终于，不可能成为了可能，我可以依靠拐杖走路了。

任何一点身体的不便都可能让人萎靡不振。虽然我依旧需要拐杖，但是残疾并没有给生活造成解决不了的障碍，恰恰相反，战胜残疾这件事给了我成就感和自信心，让我积极、勇敢地面对人生的挑战。我把在梦里才敢想的事情变成了现实，这对我的性格产生了巨大的影响。

20
摆脱恐惧的撑竿一跳

I've never been much of an athlete. I love participating in sports and I enjoy competition, but asking me to do anything besides running in a straight line has never yielded stellar results. For this reason, I was a sprinter on my high school's track team. In my junior year, the coach asked for volunteers for the pole vault, specifically sprinters who were relatively compact in stature and light in weight. This described me perfectly, and I did not have enough muscle for the shot put (or the javelin, or the discus, or the hammer throw), so I figured I would give it a try.

After practicing for a month, I had scrapes all over my legs from falling on the ground. I had knocked the wind out of myself on several occasions when the pole rebounded into my chest, and, in one nearly successful attempt, had hit my head on the bar right before I fell back to earth (and by earth, I mean the hard, rocky ground). My near misses, I was told, were because I was hesitant; I was letting fear of failing and falling get the best of me. I needed to just go for it, to forget about the potential pain, and trust myself. I kept practicing.

I remember the day I actually made it over the bar. I took ten quick measured steps, pole in hand. On the eleventh, I slowly lowered the pole toward the ground. On the twelfth, I jammed it into the ground, pushing as hard as I could, and rode the pole into the air. I landed on the mat on the other side of the bar, which did not come tumbling down upon me. I stared up at the sky, dazed and amazed, and realized for the first time that the biggest boundaries I faced in my life would come from my own fears. As long as I persisted and kept a sense of humor about things that didn't necessarily come easily to me, I could never he disappointed with myself, and I'd be surprised by what I could accomplish.

点评

本篇 Essay 风趣、乐观，申请人的自知之明讨人喜欢。为了完成一开始看起来无法完成的目标，他下定决心要弥补天生缺乏的运动能力，甘愿承受许多伤痛和挫折。从文中可以看出，申请人对于批评采取“有则改之，无则加勉”的态度，这是一种成熟的态度。在文章结尾，申请人点出，他意识到生命中束缚他的唯有恐惧。申请人为了使他的 Essay 引人注意，可谓竭尽所能。撑竿跳是一项不寻常的运动，这足以让他脱颖而出。申请人的文风流畅，引人入胜。而且，申请人还在结尾段落解释了这个决定性时刻如何影响了他对生命的看法。这个转变令人印象深刻，本篇 Essay 就是用区区 300 字写出的内容丰富的好范文。

【参考译文】

我从小就算不上是运动健将。虽然我酷爱运动，也喜欢竞争，但若是让我参加“直线奔跑”之外的任何项目，也从来没有什么辉煌的成就。正因如此，我曾是高中田径队的短跑队员。高一那年，教练想找一些学生，特别是体型相对轻巧的短跑选手，自愿参加撑竿跳项目。这肯定是我呀，我的肌肉既推不动铅球，也扔不了标枪、铁饼和链球，所以我想我应该试试。

练习了一个月之后，我的双腿满是因为摔落在地而造成的伤痕。好几次，长竿反弹在我的胸口上，痛得我喘不过气来。有一次差点成功，但头部正撞在横竿上，使我又摔回了地面（这里的地面可是坚硬的石面）。他们告诉我，每次离成功差一点都是因为我犹豫不决：我让对失败和落地的恐惧情绪控制了自己。我需要放手一搏，忘记可能的伤痛，相信自己。我不停地练啊练！

还记得我正式跃过横竿的那一天。我手拿撑竿，按事先测量的距离迅速跑了 10 步。第 11 步，我缓缓地朝地面方向压低撑竿。第 12 步，我将它插入地面，用力向前推。我乘竿而起，之后落在了横竿对面的垫子上，而且横竿没有跌落在我身上。我凝视着天空，有点眩晕，也有点惊讶。我第一次意识到，我一生中面临的最大的障碍源自我内心的恐惧。只要我坚持不懈，乐观面对那些我不擅长的事情，我就永远不会对自己失望，反而会惊叹于自己的成就。

21
弟弟自杀所带来的警醒

I picked up the telephone one Wednesday this April and immediately knew something was wrong from the tone of my second brother's voice. My youngest brother had tried to take his life. He lay in the hospital but didn't want our parents to find out. He had been clinically depressed for some time, but had said nothing to any of us. His words, his actions, and the results of the tests administered all indicated that he would probably try again.

That call shocked me. The following months have changed my approach to life.

I found the ensuing two weeks emotionally and physically draining. I spent sleepless nights deciding whether to tell my parents. I also struggled to reconcile the fact that my actions have not always reflected my personal priorities. My mind dwelt on the number of times I had put work before a call to my brothers, or a visit to my parents in West Yorkshire. The event made me acutely aware of the trade-offs I have made and continue to make. At the moment my family needs my support, yet at the same time work is entering a critical phase. I therefore spend less time with friends. I am aware of the need to constantly reassess what my priorities are.

I also found it very difficult to accept that I had missed the signs of my brother's depression. I thought I understood him because we share the same family and have had similar experiences. If I could miss something like this with my own brother, with whom I have a familial bond, how can I ever be sure of my impact on those who I know less well? I now think more deeply about all my relationships, both personal and work, and consider how my words and actions will be understood from their perspective.

点评

本篇 Essay 没有从正面描写申请人，讲述的也不是申请人克服巨大障碍的故事，但字里行间流露出的真情实感却让读者感受颇多。当申请人写到自己忽视了弟弟的抑郁症时，我们能感受到他的痛苦；当申请人努力寻找生活的真正意义时，我们与他共同努力。即使我们无法同申请人共同经历那一刻，但我们在情感上也是相通的。

这是一篇非常有力道的文章，原因显而易见。之所以入选，是因为它是申请人坦露私事的优秀范例。这也是一篇有趣的范文，因为本文没有像多数 Essay 那样选择干脆、利落的收尾方式，也没有给故事硬安上一个积极、圆满的结尾。尽管如此，这件事对申请人人格的影响仍然跃然纸上。他看上去成熟稳重，并且由于这段经历，更显其自知之明。

【参考译文】

今年四月的一个星期三，我接到二弟打来的电话。一听他的口气，我就知道出事了。最小的弟弟自杀未遂，住进了医院，但又不想让我们的父母知道。这个弟弟患抑郁症已经有些时日，却从未对我们提起过。他的言行以及专业测试的结果都表明，他很可能再次尝试自杀。

这个电话把我惊懵了。接下来的几个月改变了我的生活态度。

我感觉随后的两个星期，自己精疲力竭。我彻夜失眠，考虑应不应该告诉父母。我不断地做着心理斗争，迫使自己接受这个事实：我并不总是做自己优先考虑的事。很多次，我因为忙于工作而忘了给弟弟们打电话，或者忘记回西约克郡看望父母。这件事让我意识到，自己已经在工作和家庭中间作出取舍，而且这会是持续的决定。此刻，家人需要我的陪伴，而我的工作正进入关键阶段。因此，我减少了和朋友相处的时间。我意识到自己必须不断审视我所应该优先考虑的事情。

另一方面，我难以接受自己忽视了弟弟的抑郁症这一点。我自以为理解他，因为我们俩拥有共同的家庭背景和相似的经历。如果我自己的亲弟弟，一个与我有血缘关系的人我都可能忽略，那么又怎能确定自己对那些不熟悉的人产生的影响呢？如今，无论是私人关系还是工作关系，我的理解都更加深刻，也会换位思考别人如何理解我的言行。

22
时隔 6 个月的两次降落，见证个人成长

The 747 banked sharply to its left, its wing seemingly inches from clipping an apartment complex. I was on my way home to Hong Kong from a holiday in Taiwan. Six months earlier, in July 1997, the approach to Kai Tak had terrified me. Landing at Kai Tak was, even for a veteran flier, harrowing; pilots had to dodge buildings, turn at the last possible moment and then land on a narrow runway jutting into the harbor.

That first flight scared me, though, not just because I was unfamiliar with the steep turn but also because I was, quite literally, flying into the unknown. I was moving to Hong Kong from Washington, D.C. where I had lived for five years. I did not have a job, I did not speak Cantonese, and I knew (barely) one person, a family friend who had said I could house-sit for a month while he was in the U.S.. I would like to think I arrived in Hong Kong craving adventure but the truth is I was apprehensive and not sure I could pull it off.

Fast-forward six months to that flight from Taipei: as the plane landed I thought, "Wow, I'm home." That idea (that Hong Kong could be "home") surprised me but also made me realize how much I had grown in those six months. I had sweated through a steamy Hong Kong summer; I had turned my one contact into a network of acquaintances; I had used that network to find a job as a reporter for *Time* magazine; and, perhaps most important, I had proven I could survive—no, thrive—in a city vastly different from those I had known in the States. I was proud of myself, but not just because I had learned to live in Hong Kong. I was proud because I was confident and curious and eager to gobble up everything Hong Kong had in store for me.

点评

本篇 Essay 构思巧妙，表现了个人的成长。时隔 6 个月的两次降落，在文中构成了漂亮的平行结构，形成对比。乍一看，本文可能略显简单、琐碎——如何习惯启德机场的降落、如何习惯香港的生活，但这样的解读未免太过浅显。申请人在文中表达了他愿意承担风险，并且有能力在看上去无法战胜的挑战面前坚持不懈。申请人在职场中的成就，以及他能称香港为“家”，这些都有力地展现了他的主动性和对新环境的适应能力。在读到结尾时，我们可以想象申请人是一位个性顽强的人，渴望体验新的环境，绝不安于现状。

申请人对“决定性时刻”这个概念进行了有趣的发挥。他没有聚焦在某个具体的时刻，而是用飞机降落作为线索，描述了自己为期 6 个月的学习和个人发展之旅。尽管这样做有点剑走偏锋，但效果非常不错。

【参考译文】

波音 747 飞机向左急转，机翼似乎马上就要撞上最近的公寓楼了。我就坐在飞机上，刚从台湾度完假回香港的家。6 个月前，也就是 1997 年 7 月，在启德机场的降落让我胆战心惊。其实对于一个富有经验的老飞行员来说，在启德机场降落也可算作是一次痛苦的经历：飞行员需要避开建筑物，在最后一刻急转，然后降落在凸入港口的狭窄跑道上。

那次飞行是我来香港的第一次飞行。之所以让我害怕，并不只是因为我不熟悉飞机急转，确切地说，还因为我正在飞向完全陌生的地方——从生活了 5 年的华盛顿搬去香港。我没有工作，也不会说粤语，只认识（几乎算不上认识）一个人。他是一位家族朋友，在美国时曾答应让我在他家住一个月。我希望说服自己：来香港是因为自己渴望冒险，但事实是，我忧心忡忡，不确定自己能不能扛过去。

很快，6个月就要过去了。这次从台北度假回来，在飞机落地的时候，心中“哇，到家了”这个想法让我自己大吃一惊。同时，也让我意识到，我在6个月的时间里成长了多少。我熬过了汗流浃背的香港夏日；从只有一个联系人到拥有一张人际网，并利用这张人际网为自己在《时代周刊》找到了一份记者的工作；而最重要的也许是，我证明了自己能够在一个完全不同于美国的环境中活下来——不，茁壮成长。我为自己感到骄傲，但并不仅仅因为我学会了如何在香港生活，还因为我自信、好奇，热切地接受香港为我准备的一切。

EXPERIENCING A SETBACK OR A FAILURE

命题 4 失败的体验

Describe a setback, disappointment, or occasion of failure that you have experienced. How did you manage the situation, and what did you learn from it?

讲述你经历过的一段挫折、失望或失败的经历。说明你是如何应对那些情况的，以及你从中学到了什么。

解题思路

如果你不费吹灰之力就得到了你想要的一切，那么生活将会多么无聊。这个命题考察的就是你如何面对逆境，需要注意的是：无论你经历过怎样的挫折，请把它转变成积极的东西。不要在描述你如何失望上花费太多笔墨，尽管你需要生动地传达当时的失望之情；也请重点描述你是如何解决这个问题的，以及你从中学到了什么。

下面几篇经典 Essay 就是极好的范例。这些申请人正是这么写的——他们对当时处境的回应传达了主动性、适应性、自我意识和坚强不息。这些事件有大有小。你在挑选素材时，无须为找不到一段惊世骇俗的故事而焦虑。这道命题考察的是你对自身的理解和反省，并非事件的规模。你没有必要把自己刻画成一只涅槃重生的凤凰。

要求讲述失败经历的命题并不是为了挖掘你性格的弱点，相反，它是为了更全面地展示你的个性。Essay 的结构应尽量简单，上下文层次要有递进关系：挫折、后果、教训、解决办法以及你的心得体会等。

我们都曾经历过失败，都曾被抛弃过，都曾考砸过……我们应该感谢这一切。失败意味着你尝试了，而勇气体现在从错误中学习的能力上。你可以借这篇 Essay 来展示你如何重新复出，找到新的对手并赢得胜利。英国的杰出领袖温斯顿·丘吉尔曾说过："失败的困境是胜利的机遇。"请用你的经历向我们证明，你也相信这句话。

点评人： 贾明·埃迪斯（Jamyn Edis）

23
领导风格需因人而异

A scaffold bolt had just whistled past my ear. It was my third day on a construction site and I had been assigned six men to complete the foundations. I was only twenty years old and lacked experience and confidence, which the men were exploiting. By the end of the week, another engineer had replaced me.

My first reaction was relief, but that was soon replaced by boredom with my new filing duties. I realized that my lack of training and experience had meant that I wasn't ready to manage a team. I met with the site manager and asked to shadow another engineer for the next two weeks to learn how to lead on a construction site.

I quickly learned the basic technical aspects of the role, but, more importantly, I recognized that the other engineers had a directive style, in contrast to my desire to lead by consensus. My problems had been largely caused by my leadership style, which had not been appropriate for the situation and which I had not adjusted appropriately.

After two weeks, I persuaded the site manager to give me another team. At the start of this role I adopted an authoritative manner, which was similar to that expected by the team of laborers. Once I had developed a working relationship of mutual respect with the team, I was able to relax some aspects of the direct management approach and build a rapport with the men.

This experience allowed me to practice different leadership styles and to understand the need to adapt my approach to suit the situation, the individual, and the team. I also learned about the role of confidence and credibility when leading a team, as well as the importance of training and mentoring for new starters.

点评

申请人在讲述工作挫折时，用精心设计的旁白道出中肯的经验教训。故事用“一颗螺母从耳边呼啸飞过”这个细节开场，力量非凡，给文章增添了一丝活力和戏谑。到首段末尾，我们了解了事情的来龙去脉，也清楚了申请人所面临的挫折。

故事迅速展开，申请人简明扼要地提出了解决方案的框架——这是此类命题最重要的元素。然后进一步分析他取得的进步，说明行为在转变，处事在日渐成熟。让申请人脱颖而出的是他的自我意识和快速学习能力，由此证明了他具有极强的适应能力。文章最后归结为领导风格的进步，此乃明智之举，所有申请哈佛商学院的Essay都应表达这样的主题。

这是一篇非常有分量的文章。结构严谨，思路清晰，并且由合理的情节展现出得到的经验教训。申请人可以删去最后两段中的一些累赘描述，代之以具体事例来说明他如何在工地之外——不管是其他工作环境还是个人生活中，运用这些经验教训。

【参考译文】

一颗螺母从我耳边呼啸飞过。这是我到工地上班的第三天。作为一名监工，公司给我分派了6个工人，我要监督他们完成打地基的工作。我刚满20岁，初出茅庐，一副怯生生的样子，那帮人正好利用了这一点——到了周末，我被另一名监工替换掉了。

我的第一反应是长舒了一口气，但很快就被整理文档这项新工作给烦透了。我想，之前失败的原因可能是我一没经验，二没受训，因此无法管理团队。我找到工地经理，要求接下来两周，让我跟随其他监工学习如何督导工地。

我很快学会了这个职位所需的基础技术知识，但更重要的是，我发现其他监工的领导风格是命令式的，与我总想与工人达成一致的风格相反。我之前的问题在很大程度上要归咎于我的领导风格，它不适合这类工作场合，而我也没有作出适当调整。

两周后，我说服工地经理再给我一支队伍。刚上任时我独断专行，这和那群工人预想得差不多。在与他们建立了相互尊重的工作关系之后，我就在某些方面放宽了自己命令式的领导方式，与他们和睦相处。

我在这段经历中尝试了各种领导方式，懂得了领导风格需因地制宜，因人而异。我还学到了信心和威望在领导团队时的作用，另外，培训指点新人也很重要。

24
巧妙解决文化与性别歧视

My first project at Accenture consisted of an SAP implementation for Chile's largest copper mining company. Thanks to the experience I had acquired on the human resources module, I was asked to train the geographical divisions' personnel. I had spent several days preparing the training material and rehearsing, when I arrived to the Chuquicamata site, the largest open sky mine in the world, where forty administrative staff and supervisors were expecting me for weeklong training. They were all men and most of them former miners. The first session was terrible! I did not get any attention from my audience, and they were even disrespectful toward me.

There is a strong cultural rivalry between Chile and Argentina, to the point that some Chilean clients refuse to be served by Argentinean consulting teams. Additionally, very few women work in Chile, and even fewer are executives. That day, I had the feeling I was paying for both being an Argentinean and a woman. However, I was extremely disappointed with my own performance and incapacity to control the group.

Toward the late afternoon, I interrupted the formal session and opened up the dialogue, reinforcing why I thought this training was important for all participants, and how it would affect their daily work. I also clearly stated how unprofessional their attitude had been and how it made me feel. After discussing what they wanted to get out of the training, we agreed on having eight extra hours to compensate for the time lost. From that moment on the group's attitude changed radically, my role was accepted and the training turned out to be a great success.

What I learned from this episode was above all the absolute imperative to adapt the message and format of any presentation to its audience, and to identify and address the potential sources of conflict up front.

点评

申请人发现自己陷入了困境。很多职场人士都会遇到类似的情况：来到陌生的环境、感觉能力不足、遇到有敌意的客户。申请人提供了许多细节，让读者自然而然地同情她身为一个女人所面临的文化歧视和性别歧视。字数有限，因此不能在背景描述上花费过多的笔墨，但讲述一个能让大家感同身受的故事至关重要。

在接下来的描述中，申请人一步步地解释了她的三点行动计划，然后评估她如何改变自己的处境。正如大多数描写失败经历的经典Essay一样，最后的结果是积极的。申请人向读者证明了，无论形势多么紧迫，她都有能力以成熟而理性的态度应对挫折。

【参考译文】

我在埃森哲公司做的第一个项目是为智利最大的铜矿企业实施SAP系统。由于我具备人力资源模型方面的相关经验，我被调去培训地质部门的工作人员。我花了几天时间准备培训材料，并预先模拟。等我到了世界上最大的露天矿场丘基卡马塔矿场（Chuquicamata）时，那里的40位行政人员和主管已经等着我进行为期一周的培训了。他们都是清一色的男人，大部分人以前是矿工。第一堂培训课简直糟糕极了！完全没有人听我培训，他们甚至还对我出言不逊。

智利和阿根廷之间存在着严重的文化冲突，以至于一些智利客户甚至拒绝接受阿根廷咨询公司的服务。而且，在智利，参加工作的女人凤毛麟角，高层管理人员更是寥寥无几。那天，我觉得，我是在为自己身为女人及阿根廷人而付出代价。不过，我更为自己糟糕的控场表现感到失望。

下午快结束时，我停止了培训的内容，开始和学员们对话。我向他们强调

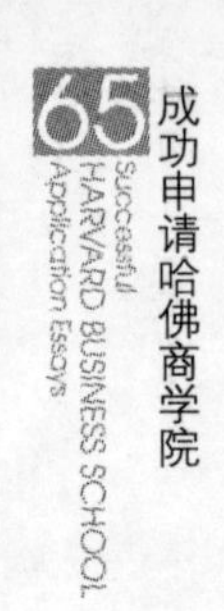

了这次培训对所有参与者的重要性，以及它会如何影响他们的日常工作。我还清楚地指出，他们之前的态度是多么缺乏职业素养，并向他们表达出我的感受。在讨论了他们对这次培训的要求之后，我们一致同意再额外增加 8 个小时以弥补损失的时间。从那一刻起，学员们的态度发生了根本性的变化，他们接受了我的角色，而培训也取得了极大的成功。

从此次事件中我了解到，传达信息之前，首先要根据受众调整你想要呈现的信息以及呈现方式，确定并解决潜在的冲突来源。

25
寻求内心力量以克服顽疾

One of my greatest struggles has been with my speech. I had a stuttering problem from age four that was a constant source of self-doubt until recently. In fourth grade, my parents took me to a speech pathologist in Houston who, through a yearlong program, "cured" my stuttering. After Exxon hired me in 1997, I experienced a demoralizing failure of speech that made me realize my stuttering was definitely not cured.

The cost engineering section had gathered to update our new worldwide manager on current projects and initiatives. We were supposed to introduce ourselves and summarize our activities. When it came time for my introduction, I turned toward him, reached out my hand in greeting and said, "I'm J…" As I tried to say my name, my vocal cords locked. For what seemed like an eternity, I tried to force my way past the block, but the embarrassed stares from my peers and supervisors just increased my paralysis. Eventually, I made it through the introduction and work summary but not before having that experience burned in my memory. Immediately after that incident, I started searching for a "miracle" drug to cure stuttering. After a few frustrating months, I realized that no cure existed so I purchased a self-help book. I practiced the exercises for several months and noticed some improvement in my speech, but when disfluencies still occurred, I felt helpless. After two more years of avoiding difficult speaking situations, I consulted the Stuttering Foundation of America, which made me understand that stuttering is something that can never be completely cured but can be managed through self-awareness. To gain awareness of my stuttering, I have been keeping a daily journal of my speech habits. I document how my speech muscles react in stuttering situations and practice modifying or relaxing those muscles in similar situations. My newfound control over my speech has led me to actively seek out speaking situations that I avoided before. For instance, I was elected president of my homeowners' association, and I have shared several safety learnings in front of the sixty employees in my department. As my success grows, so, too, does my confidence to where I rarely experience speech blocks like I did in 1997. However, I've realized that I must practice, practice, practice and that I will be doing this the rest of my life.

While the concept of practice makes perfect isn't new, it has taken on new meaning for how I lead my life. I know that every aspect of my life where I'd like to see improvement must involve a substantial amount of practice, from negotiating skills to surfing, from networking with colleagues to training my dog.

点评

申请人非常勇敢地和大家分享了一段他亲身经历过的重大挑战，以及他征服挑战的过程。简单说明自己的口吃问题后，申请人马上切入了那极度痛苦的一刻：他正面临他自以为克服多年的障碍。作为读者，你满怀同情，希望他成功。不过，本文可不是催泪弹。你在撰写 Essay 时也要小心，别为了赚取廉价的同情分讲悲情故事（因为你赚不到）。申请人尴尬万分，我们感同身受，但不会无故给予怜悯。

申请人积极地拟定自助计划和寻求外部建议，这表明他下定了决心。接着，申请人又举例说明了他按教程练习，以及不努力练习一定一事无成的领悟。申请人给出的结论虽然初看肤浅，但是它抓住了一篇陈述失败经历的优秀文章的本质，即寻找内心的力量以克服障碍，无论它是多么得令人畏惧。

【参考译文】

我经历过的最艰苦的斗争之一是矫正口吃。4 岁那年，我患上口吃，而直至最近，口吃一直是我缺乏自信的根源。上四年级时，父母带我去休斯敦一位语言病理学家处就医。经过一年的治疗，他矫正了我的口吃。1997年加入埃克森公司后，我又一次令人沮丧地在说话时“卡壳”了。我意识到自己的口吃毛病并没有“痊愈”。

新任全球经理刚刚上任，召集工程成本核算部门的各位员工向他报告目前的项目进展和新计划。流程是每个人先作自我介绍，然后总结手头的项目。轮到我时，我转过身，伸手向他问候道：“我叫约……”声带突然在我自报家门时打结了。那一刻，时间仿佛静止了，我竭力逼自己突破障碍，但在同事和主管们的注视下，我感到万分尴尬，越发结巴起来。最后，我终于完成了自我介绍和工作总结，但这段经历却深深地烙印在我的记忆中。那次事件后不久，我开始寻访“灵丹妙药”以医治口吃。经过令人沮丧的数月时间，我意识到根本就没有特效药，于是我买了一本自助书籍。按照里面的指导练习了几个月，说话终于顺畅多了，可仍然难免有磕巴的时候，我无望极了。在我避开重大的演讲场合两年多后，我咨询了美国口吃基金会，了解到口吃是永远无法痊愈的顽疾，但可以通过自我意识加以控制。为了解决我的口吃毛病，我养成了每天记录自己讲话的习惯。记录在口吃时，语言表达所需的肌肉是如何运动的，然后练习在那种情况下如何调整、放松肌肉。新方法让我主动争取以前避之不及的发言机会。例如，我被选为业主协会会长，为业主们争取权益；我还在本部门60位员工面前分享安全知识等。随着我越来越成功地克服口吃，我也越来越自信了，我相信1997年那次经历再也不会发生了。不过，我也知道我需要不停地练习，而且这一辈子我都会这样练习下去。

虽然熟能生巧是老生常谈，但它给我的生活赋予了全新的含义。我知道，无论是从谈判技巧到冲浪，还是从工作中的人际交往到训练我的爱犬，要想改善生活中的任何方面，都需要大量的实践。

26

以职业精神处理公司解散的善后事务

In the course of only a few months, my Bain colleague Graham and I transformed ChangeAddress.com from an idea into a company. We raised $1.8 million in venture funding led by multibillion-dollar Cox Enterprises, brought together a powerful and motivated board (including a former postmaster general and chief of staff under Lyndon Johnson) and hired nineteen incredibly talented individuals. We built the most feature-rich and user-friendly online address change service available to the forty-four million annual U.S. movers.

By the late fall of 2000, revenues were growing nearly 50 percent month-to-month. This was not, however, sufficient to cover our cash burn rate. Though we had allocated resources with significant conservatism, we had always known that we would need an additional round of approximately $5 million to generate positive operating cash flows. In a series of frustrating setbacks, several strategic and venture capital investors pulled back their once overwhelming interest, leaving us with dissolution as our only option.

Despite our profound feelings of loss, Graham and I approached the wind-down with the same degree of professionalism and courage as our initial fund-raising. We identified every stakeholder involved in our business, and made a joint decision that the welfare of our employees would come first and our personal financial considerations would come last. We leveraged our network of Atlanta business contacts to help each of our workers find jobs and arranged to sell the assets of the company to our business partner, Moving.com, for enough money to avoid bankruptcy and return some money to our preferred shareholders.

Despite the financial failure, the learning experience from ChangeAddress.com transcends the dollars and cents—Graham and I learned how to inspire a group of individuals to follow a vision and create something out of nothing. And we learned that, despite the risks and uncertainties we face, the only true mistake is to be afraid to make one.

点评

本篇范文正是描述失败经历的好范文。本文展示了申请人的干劲、适应能力，以及其正直的品行。而且，这些品德都点缀在一个引人入胜的故事里，在文章深度和切题之间达成了平衡。这篇 Essay 的结构紧凑——开篇、中段、结尾，是非常基础的故事结构。

一开始，申请人就描绘了对许多准 MBA 学生来说非常熟悉的一幕。申请人并非头脑发热、好高骛远的人，相反，他深切关心为他工作的人，为自己让他们失望而深表遗憾，博取了大家的同情。申请人深知自己的失败让很多股东受到了影响，而且他深知自己对股东的信用义务。他将自己的财务补偿放在最后，这显示了申请人惊人的成熟度，让读者感觉这些品德会伴随他整个职业生涯。

【参考译文】

在短短几个月的时间内，我和贝恩公司的同事格雷厄姆将 ChangeAddress 网站从一个点子变成了一家公司。我们筹集了高达 180 万美元的风险投资基金，由资产数十亿的考克斯公司挑头，组成了一个强大而热情高涨的董事会（包括林登·约翰逊总统手下的前邮电部部长和总参谋长），还雇用了 19 位才华横溢的员工。我们打造了一个最富有特色、最易于使用的在线地址变更平台，为每年 4 400 万的美国搬家人士提供服务。

到 2000 年深秋，公司的总收入以接近 50% 的速度逐月递增。然而，这样的收入仍不足以弥补我们的现金耗费。虽然我们之前一直以极其保守的态度来分配资源，但还需要筹集约 500 万美元才能维持现金流的健康周转。经历了一系列令人沮丧的挫折之后，几家战略风险投资人失去了兴趣，撤走了原先的资金，留给我们的只剩下解散这条路。

尽管难掩心中的失落之情，我和格雷厄姆依然以当初募资时的职业精神以及勇气来处理善后事务。我们与每一位参与的股东协商后一致作出决定：员工的利益排在第一位，我们个人的财务放在最后。我们利用在亚特兰大的业务往来关系网帮每一位员工找到了工作，并将公司财产变卖给我们生意上的合作伙伴moving网站，从而得到了足够的资金以避免破产，还退还了原始股东一部分钱。

虽然我们在财务上失败了，但是，从这次创业经历中学到的东西远超过金钱。我和格雷厄姆学会了怎样激励团队去追求一个愿景，怎样从零开始创造。我们还意识到，尽管我们面临风险和不确定因素，但唯一真正的错误是害怕犯错误。

27
必要的改变何时都不晚

Time never passes more slowly than when waiting for an actor to remember his next line. During my senior year in high school I earned the opportunity to direct a play from casting to curtain call. However, what should have been a pleasant, two-and-a-half-hour performance turned into a four-hour ordeal. I honestly felt sorry for the audience.

I did not realize the problems my casting had caused until two weeks before the show when the lead actress was suspended and the lead actor was still using cue cards he had hidden around the set. I should have mitigated my poor evaluation of my cast by replacing the lead actress and adapting my directing style to reap the talent of my lead actor. Instead, I continued with my plan, confident that my two actors would pull themselves together. The lead actress assured me she would be ready for the show, and the lead actor, who later went to Juilliard, would surely perform to his skill level.

My confidence was shattered that first long performance. My mistake was in my casting, but my failure was in my unwillingness to make the changes the play needed to succeed. This experience strengthened my skills in critically evaluating the strengths of my team members, but the lesson that has haunted me is that it is never too late to change direction when success demands it.

Years later, when I re-created the process monitoring system at the Koch refinery, the first version was complete when I realized that major revisions were needed to keep the system running after I was gone; I had to change direction. I spent two months working extra hours to complete the revisions. Six months later, my assistance has not once been needed to maintain or operate the system.

点评

想到演员们在台上一句句挤台词，你都能感受到申请人在台下如坐针毡。申请人不失时机地讲述了一个不落俗套的有关个人失败经历的例子。从本文可以看出，并非一定要写和工作相关的故事。事实上，许多人的故事都与工作无关。不过，千万记得要将你学到的东西跟你上商学院的动机联系起来。

文中，申请人有意通过一堆“本应该”、“将会”、“有可能”这样的词语传达他的主要收获，表明自己是多么希望采取了行动。这一点满足了该话题对个人学习能力的要求，也让读者相信，主人公确实吸取了教训。此外，文章巧妙引出下一个例子，表现他如何将经验教训应用在科克炼油厂的项目上。文章表现申请人创造性和商业意识的篇幅各占一半，显示出他是一个全面发展的人。

【参考译文】

再也没有比等待演员记起下一句台词更漫长的时刻了。读高中时，我争取到导演一部戏剧的机会，包括从选演员到谢幕的所有工作。那本该是一场两个半小时的愉快演出，但最终却变成了长达 4 个小时的噩梦。我真诚地向观众表示歉意。

直到正式上演前两个星期，我才发现演员有问题。当时女主角罢演，而男主角还需要用事先藏在道具周围的台词提示卡。要是我能够早点换掉女主角，并且调整导演风格以发挥男主角的天分的话，也许还有可能弥补选角的错误。但事实上,我任其发展,以为两位演员会齐心协力准备这出戏。女主角向我保证，她会好好准备的；而男主角也保证会充分发挥自己的水平（后来他去了茱莉亚音乐学院）。

第一场漫长的演出结束后，我的信心被击碎了。我的错误犯在选角不当，可导致演出最终失败的原因是我不愿做必要的调整来扭转形势。那次事件确实提高了我严格评估队员实力的技能，但令我刻骨铭心的教训是，如果要想成功就必须改变方向，而任何时候改变都不晚。

多年以后，我在为科克炼油厂重新设计流程监控系统时发现，要想系统能够在无人监控的条件下维持正常运行，需要大幅改动。当时，第一个版本已经设计完成，但我不得不调转方向。为了完成修改，我加班加点地工作了两个月。值得高兴的是，6个月后，我的助手一次都不用去操作或维修该系统了。

28
为快速调整而喝彩

We had one thousand children and one hundred counselors on a cruise ship bound to Alaska. The project was the Young Presidents Organization family cruise, and I was contracted to help coordinate the youth activities under difficult constraints—space, time, and resources being the greatest of these.

To provide our clients with a memorable experience, we built a system that was capable of manipulating thousands of variables (staff, space, time, budget) into a solution that would allow each child maximum exposure to his or her favorite activity.

This solution was so complex that it confused the parents, children, and our staff alike. Extreme dissatisfaction emanated only three hours into our 168-hour contract. The project lead looked to me to uncover the source of our problem, as well as provide and implement the appropriate solution.

By hour twelve we had regrouped and redrawn our approach with a new understanding. Our objective was to ensure that each child went to bed with a smile; it was not to provide a custom adventure. Children were less worried about what they were doing, than who they were with—fun, motivated counselors in an environment that included friends. We achieved tremendous success, resulting in accolades not only for our service delivery, but also for our flexibility and quick turnaround.

I learned that it is important to fully understand the client and her/his end objectives. Additionally, it is important to deliver a solution that is complex enough to meet those needs—but no more. We had spent too much time engineering the solution, and not enough understanding the problem. What seemed like a new and innovative approach was just a complicated, difficult, and time-consuming method of delivering fun.

点评

申请人讲了一个勇于承认错误、甘愿放弃之前的辛勤成果而立刻重新开始的好故事。申请人没能解决他遇到的难题，而是承认失败，用一个简单的方案应对问题，这表现出申请人的创造性和灵活性。结果是，虽然他原本的计划未能按预期进行，但他能够力挽狂澜，避免了整个游船项目的彻底失败。

本文的节奏控制得当，框架结构分明，并从中传递了中心内容：背景、问题、解决方法以及心得体会。尽管你可以任意采用写作格式，但由于字数受限，你不应该太偏离基本框架。给你一个忠告：以负面描写作为结尾会给读者留下“失败是无可挽回”的印象。本篇 Essay 则不是，申请人在最后一段揭示了他学到的经验教训。不过，除非你有充足的理由，不然最好以正面叙述结尾。

【参考译文】

在一艘开往阿拉斯加的游轮上共有 1 000 名儿童和 100 位辅导员。这是青年总裁协会（YPO）家庭游轮项目。我受雇在有限条件下帮助协调青少年活动，其中，空间、时间和资源是最大的困难。

为了给我们的客户留下难忘的经历，我们设计了一套系统，它能够将各种变量（员工、空间、时间，以及预算）巧妙地结合，从而形成一个解决方案，让每位孩子能最大程度地参与他最喜欢的活动。

但是，这个方案过于复杂，使家长和孩子都无法理解，就连我们的工作人员都不太明白。短短三小时之后，家长就对我们 168 小时的合同提出了不满。项目领导指望我找出问题的症结所在，提供恰当的解决方案并加以执行。

12个小时之后，我们重新分组，按照新的思路规划我们的方案。我们的目标是确保每个小朋友都带着笑容入睡，而不再是提供订制的冒险经历。孩子们并不在意他们干什么，他们更在乎和谁在一起——好玩且热情高涨的辅导员，以及一个拥有朋友的环境。我们获得了圆满的成功，不仅提供的服务得到了赞美，客户更为我们的灵活性和快速调整能力喝彩。

我认识到，充分理解客户以及他的最终目标非常重要。另外，提供一个满足需求的复杂方案，但不要过分复杂。我们花了太多时间设计方案，却没有充分了解问题所在：那些看上去新颖而富有创意的方案，不过是复杂、繁琐、浪费时间的娱乐方式而已。

29
克制对个人荣誉的渴望

I had just arrived in my unit, fresh from the U.S. Army Ranger School and the officer basic course, when my company set out on a twelve-mile foot march. By mile five, my radioman fell out of formation, unable to carry the extra weight of the radio along with the normal seventy pounds. Anxious to make a good impression, I eagerly took on his burden.

Around mile eight, I myself started running out of breath. I refused Sergeant Nelson's offer of help, determined to conquer this obstacle with tenacity, determination, and the stubborn refusal to give up. I marched for another two miles, hyperventilating each step of the way. Then, to my supreme embarrassment, I passed out. The platoon sauntered by me, their stricken platoon leader, as I lay along the side of the road while my sergeants doused canteen water on my groggy head.

I failed because of my pride. It was a lesson that would lead to a fundamental shift in my understanding of leadership. Instead of trying to be the hero of my platoon, I soon learned to accept the help of my sergeants. The ultimate success of the platoon depended on the actions of my squad and team leaders. The reserve of talent and potential there were far greater than anything I could have accomplished on my own. The best leaders, I learned, subsume their need for individual recognition in order to let their subordinates and superiors shine.

I changed my approach and our platoon excelled. Two months later, the battalion embarked on a twenty-five-mile foot march, a test of character and will. I marched at the head of the platoon, setting the example and encouraging the soldiers. My squad and team leaders kept their men in line, distributing the heavy equipment among themselves. Of the twenty-seven platoons in the battalion, ours was the only one of two that finished without a soldier falling out. As for the radio, between myself, the radioman, Sergeant Nelson, Sergeant Gryder, and Sergeant Brown, we all shared the burden.

点 评

"游骑兵做先锋！"是美国陆军游骑兵的座右铭。文中，申请人展示了他如何将此理念发挥到极致，结果却让手下失望。本文在强调自大、意气用事、蛮干的危险性方面表现杰出。读者在看到申请人最初的失败之后，又为他的成功喝彩。

幸好申请人没有误以为一组特别的场景足够撑起一篇文章，相反，他非常重视在失败中学习、总结，并表明该经验教训适用于各种情况。与此话题选编的其他优秀文章一样，该文章同样生气勃勃，结构严谨，引人注目，充分地展现了申请人个人的成长以及领导技能的提高。

【参考译文】

我在美国陆军游骑兵学校修完基础军官课程抵达部队时，部队组织了一次长达 19 千米的徒步行军。走了 8 千米后，团队的无线电员累得不成人样，实在背不动他的无线电台以及 3 千克重的标准配备。我迫切地想好好表现一番，于是主动地接过了他的负重。

大约走了 12 千米时，我自己也开始气喘如牛。我拒绝了纳尔逊中士的帮助，打定主意要凭着自己的意志力克服身体的疲惫。又行进了 3 千米，每走一步都气喘吁吁。接着，更令我尴尬的是，我晕倒了。我平躺在路边，士兵们用水壶浇我那颗迷迷糊糊的脑袋。整个排都因为我这个病排长耽误了行军速度。

我被骄傲打败了。正是此次教训彻底改变了我对领导者的理解。我不再逞英雄，而是学会了接受士兵们的帮助。全排的胜利靠的是小分队和班组长的齐心协力。整个团队的努力远比单枪匹马更能成大事。我发现，优秀的领导者应该克制自己对个人荣誉的渴望，让上级和下级都展露光芒。

当我改变领导方式后，我们排的成绩遥遥领先。两个月后，大队组织了一次全程 40 千米的徒步行军，这是一场性格和意志的考验。我走在全排队伍的第一个，给战士们树立榜样，鼓气加油。小分队和班组长维持队伍秩序，并轮流背负重装备。整个大队共有 27 个排，我们排是仅有的两支没有掉队士兵的队伍之一。至于那个无线电台，则由我、无线电员、纳尔逊中士、格莱德中士、布朗中士轮流负责。

30
糟糕的沟通

During my first consulting project, I was asked to construct a sales plan for an insurance company. The first step was to meet Adam, the director of sales, to discuss forecasting assumptions. A list of questions in hand, I knocked on the door. To my surprise, Adam was very formal in his reception. He did not understand why we were meeting, so I explained that I would he creating sales plans. At that point, he became outright hostile. He barked out his non-answers to my questions and informed me he was very busy… preparing sales plans. Before I could suggest cooperation, I was ushered out, and the door slammed behind me. Too shocked to react to the secretary's condescending smirk, I attempted to grasp why a textbook opportunity for teamwork became such a spectacular failure. What had I done to attract such hostility? I had just wanted to help. I called my engagement manager to complain, but he just accused me of handling the situation poorly. I was crushed and convinced that I was not cut out for consulting.

To this day, I am not sure why Adam was so hostile. Retrospectively, I can only guess that he was insulted and threatened, because no one had formally requested his assistance. Instead, a twenty-two-year-old appeared in his office, ready to perform one of his most challenging tasks.

Adam and I never became friends, but the incident profoundly affected the way I communicate. Now, every time I interview a client, I begin by exploring and allaying any fears the person might have. I explain the project's rationale and seek a frank reaction. The rapport thus established makes the interviewees comfortable enough to share private opinions. This very human interaction not only secures me with quick yet profound insights, but also relationships that often far outlast consulting projects.

点评

本篇 Essay 是一篇优秀的描写失败经历的范文，部分原因是故事主线并没有一个快乐的结局。与此相反，很多描写失败经历的 Essay 实际上都是成功事例，只是把重点放在过程中的挫折上而已。然而在本篇 Essay 中，申请人坦承他搞砸了与亚当的会面。虽然他没有直说，但我们大概能猜出他和亚当从来不曾有过具有成效的工作关系（没成为朋友无所谓）。由此可见，本文描写的是一次真正的失败经历。当你在写失败经历的 Essay 时，不要浪费时间在掩饰失败的结果上。直言事情的经过，然后继续。

当然，申请人从这次经历中学到了什么才是关键。答案是：相当多的东西。我们看到了申请人不屈不挠的精神。他最初认为自己不是做咨询的料，但他凭借这段经历，完全改变了自己与客户的沟通方式，结果是重新致力于与客户建立关系和信任。申请人曾被打败，但因为这次经历成长为擅长与高层领导者工作的更成熟的人。与上级相处的能力，以及优雅、直率地应付与各阶层员工的困难对话的能力，这些都将使申请人在哈佛商学院以及未来的职场中受益匪浅。

【参考译文】

我做的第一个咨询项目是应邀为一家保险公司设计一套销售计划。工作的第一步就是会见销售总监亚当，讨论前景预测。我手拿一份问题清单，敲开了亚当的门，但令我惊讶的是，亚当完全是出于礼节性地在接待我。他不明白我们见面的用意，于是我解释说，我的任务是设计销售计划。就在此时，他露出了明显的敌意。他冲我厉声嚷嚷，答非所问，并告诉我他很忙——忙着准备销售计划。我还来不及提议合作，就被请了出去。门在我背后“砰”的一声关上了。由于过于震惊，我连秘书那傲慢的假笑都无暇顾及。我想不明白，为什么这么一次中规中矩的团队合作竟然变成了惨败。我到底做了什么引得他大动肝火呢？我只想提供帮助！我打电话给项目经理抱怨，但他只是指责我处理事情缺乏技巧。我被打垮了，深信自己不是做咨询的料。

直到今日，我仍不知道亚当为何那么不友好。回想事情经过，我只能猜测是因为没人正式请求他的协助。相反，一个 22 岁的毛头小子出现在他的办公室里，准备完成他手上最难的任务，所以，他感觉自己受到了侮辱和威胁。

我和亚当从来没有成为朋友，但那次事件深深地影响了我的沟通方式。现在，每当我拜访客户时，我都会在一开始探察并减轻对方可能产生的恐惧感。我解释项目方案的原理，寻求直率的回应。这样建立起来的合作关系使得被拜访人能够放松心情，分享个人见解。这种人情味十足的交往不仅能让我得到敏捷而深刻的洞见，而且也使我和客户的关系比咨询项目持续得更久。

ETHICAL DILEMMA

命题 5
道德困境

Discuss an ethical dilemma that you experienced firsthand. How did you manage and resolve the situation?

讲述一段你曾亲身遭遇过的道德困境，并说明你是如何成功解决这道难题的。

解题思路

这个命题为你提供了展示能力的机会，以证明自己在责任与价值观发生冲突时如何作出艰难抉择。文章可以表现你对生活中的灰色地带——没有明确对错的事情的看法，你如何处理道德问题，以及指导原则是什么。

正如下面的范文所示，道德困境的形式可能有很多，事情发生的原委可能也很复杂。有些道德困境解决起来可能很简单，选择说真话或者撒谎即可，而有些道德困境可能要处理个人价值观与社会习俗之间的冲突。这些问题可能发生在工作上，对职业生涯产生严重影响；也可能是家庭义务方面的问题，使亲情遭受威胁。但是，无论哪种情况，这些问题意义深远，而且是一场考验。

要想得到录取委员会的青睐，申请人不仅要讲个好故事，还要写清楚导致道德困境产生的原因，以及你为什么难以抉择。为什么这对你是一场考验？一定要分析你的思考过程，以及个人道德和信仰在其中所起的作用。要诚实且个性化。此话题的要点是展现申请人的本性，如果你不敞开心扉，是无法完成这项任务的。

点评人： 安娜丽莎·巴莱尔斯（Analisa Balares）

31
坚持真理与迎合客户之间的权衡

I saw he was a banker from his pinstripes. I'd worked with bankers before, in Hong Kong. He flashed a smile.

"These numbers aren't going to work for us, son." I was sent back to "reevaluate" my projections.

It was the late'90s. The markets were buoyant, and dot-coms ruled. I was a consultant, working in Europe on a pre-IPO media company. With hindsight, floating as an online publisher was perhaps misjudged, but that was our mandate.

Working alongside bankers from a financial behemoth, we developed a model to value the company, before flotation in the U.S. and Europe. Because of the bank's deal structure, my firm had been brought in as an independent party to ratify the valuation. My responsibility was to develop a model to project the client's global businesses. I had spent two months researching, interviewing regional managers, and building the model.

Then the bankers arrived with a week of comp analysis. They suggested I alter my model to suit their estimations. They had the bigger picture, they assured me.

I was extremely uncomfortable. I told my manager I was under pressure to change my numbers, based on inadequate analysis. And this wasn't an internal business case, but a pre-IPO valuation; future shareholders would be affected. I told him I could not proceed this way with integrity. Unfortunately, I learned my team had an agenda; a technology venture was being discussed with the client. He suggested I proceed as instructed; after all, these were subjective forecasts. Balancing these considerations,

whilst acknowledging there was no "right" answer, I compromised. I said I would produce two models; one with my original forecasts, and one with the bank's figures. I would hand over both models, but leave the decision with my superiors. I passed this by my mentor, and she agreed with my approach.

Later, my mentor assured me I had acted legally and ethically and she applauded my solution and interpersonal skills. The experience taught me you cannot always convince others to act honestly; however you must always play your role with integrity. With today's headlines of corporate misconduct, this message is more relevant than ever; I always ask myself: "How would my actions play on the *WSJ* front page?"

In conclusion, I honestly don't know which numbers they used. The stock opened at $8; a year on, it hovered at $8.

Note: certain identifying information has been changed to preserve confidentiality.

点评

这篇文章非常有趣、引人入胜。但是，作为一篇讲述道德困境的短文，其成功的关键在于，文章清晰地表达了坚持真理和为客户服务两者之间的核心冲突。我们目睹申请人在似乎不可调和的矛盾之中挣扎，寻找折中的办法。他的经理没有解决问题，而是把问题抛给了他。

申请人通过本文展示了他的顽强性格，并且发表了他对个人道德的宝贵见解。申请人看上去不是一个会违背操守的人，同时也非常现实，明白直接拒绝调整预估数据不能解决问题（反而很有可能对个人职业发展造成不良后果）。毫无疑问，他有能力处理道德困境。

【参考译文】

看他穿着细条纹西服，我猜他是个银行经纪人，因为我之前和香港的银行经纪人合作过。他的脸上闪过一丝微笑。

“年轻人，这些数字对我们没用。”我的企业上市价值评估被打回来“重新”评估。

当时是 20 世纪 90 年代后期，市场一片繁荣，互联网公司一统天下。我是一家欧洲公司的咨询顾问，正忙于一家媒体公司的前期上市工作。事后看来，以在线出版商的身份上市可能属于判断失误，但那是我们的任务。

该公司在美国和欧洲上市之前，我们与一家金融巨头合作，设计模型以评估公司的价值。根据该银行的交易规范，我们公司被邀请作为独立的第三方机构来审核该公司的价值。我的职责是设计一个模型，预测客户的全球业绩。我花了两个月做研究，拜访区域经理并建模。

然后，银行经纪人带着算了一周的对比分析到了。他们建议我修改模型，迎合他们的评估，他们还向我保证说他们会通盘考虑的。

我感到忐忑不安。于是，我告诉经理，根据不充分的分析修改数据，我觉得压力很大。况且，这不是内部业务评估，而是上市前的价值评估，未来股东的收益会受到影响。我告诉他，我的职业道德不允许我这么做。可惜，我得知我们团队的议程已定，他们还在和这家客户洽谈一个科技投资项目。经理建议我按照对方的指示做修改，毕竟，这些都是主观预测。权衡各项因素，同时也认为“正确”答案反正不存在，我妥协了。我说，我会建两个模型，一个用我原先的预测数据，另一个用银行提供的数字。两个模型我都会提交，让经理们决定用哪一个。我把这件事告诉我的导师，她也同意我的做法。

后来，导师向我保证，我的做法符合法律和道德规范，她还表扬了我的解决方法和人际交往技能。这段经历让我认识到，你不可能说服每个人诚实处事，但是你必须始终坚持诚信。当如今的头条新闻充斥着对企业失当的报道，这句话比以往更有意义。我不停地扪心自问：“我的行为会如何影响《华尔街日报》的头版新闻呢？”

最终，我还是不知道他们用了哪组数据。该股开盘价为 8 元；1 年后，仍在 8 美元上下徘徊。[①]

① 为了保密，已经更改了申请人的某些身份信息。

32
拒绝用假身份调研

I walked uneasily out of my colleague's office pondering the new competitor research project he had assigned me. Jorge had asked me to assume a false identity to facilitate data gathering in market interviews. He wanted to know all of thc practices and pricing of our direct competitors.

I was uncomfortable employing these deceptive practices, but I failed to confront him. Was I naively blowing out of proportion a common business practice in Mexico? Did I have the right to apply my own ethical principles in a cultural environment with distinct norms and behaviors? Would it hinder my effectiveness if I did not follow typical local practices? Beleaguered with doubts, I delayed the calls, concentrating instead on background Internet research.

After several status inquiries from Jorge, I could not postpone the work any longer. At last, with a pit in my stomach, I dialed the first company. As the phone rang, I struggled to keep my "story" straight: my "pseudonym," my "company," and the accompanying contact information. At last I heard a voice. Perspiring and uneasy, I hung up the phone. Conducting sound business should not be this trying—my personal convictions won out.

I blocked out an appointment to meet with a former consultant of the competitor firm I had tried calling. It turned out that she was able to provide me with the same relevant and timely data I was seeking, without breaking her own confidentiality agreements. I quickly drew up a report of this company based on my in-house interview and Internet research. Armed with this deliverable and my reinforced convictions, I walked into Jorge's office.

I was frank with him about my discomfort at making the competitor calls under a false identity. Whether or not it was an accepted Mexican practice, I did not feel it was an ethically responsible activity for a large multinational consulting firm to be undertaking. I proposed my approach of using Internet tools and our colleagues to obtain as much legitimate data as possible, acknowledging the importance of this market intelligence for making product, pricing, and promotion decisions.

Though initially disappointed with my reticence, Jorge valued my openness and recognized the potential risks in his plan. He agreed to follow my alternate approach. Instead of hurting our relationship, it fostered greater confidence and respect. He knows he can count on me to get the job done—but he also knows I will stand up for my beliefs.

点评

本篇 Essay 描写的又是一桩在工作职责和个人价值观之间起冲突的事例。这一问题尤为复杂，因为这个有道德争议的职场行为，似乎是墨西哥企业的惯例。有些人可能就是利用这一点为自己向原则妥协的行为而辩解，但申请人办不到，他在第一次尝试撒谎时几乎产生了生理上的不适。

他拒绝用假身份这一行为证实了他的价值观，同时发现了一个合乎道德标准的替代方案，这证明了他有能力在其道德规范之内达到他的目标。而且，文中大量的细节及真实的情感描绘使故事更具可信度。

【参考译文】

我不安地走出同事的办公室，揣摩着他新分派给我的竞争对手调研项目。乔治要我用假身份推动市场调研中的数据收集，因为他想知道我们的直接竞争对手的所有市场活动和价格。

我对采用这些欺骗伎俩感到不安，但没敢当面提出来。是不是我太天真了，把在墨西哥习以为常的生意手段当成天大的问题？我有权在一个截然不同的规范和行为的文化环境里应用我自己的道德标准吗？如果我不遵守当地的惯例，会影响我的工作效率吗？由于疑虑重重，我推迟了电话调研，而只是在互联网上调查一些背景信息。

乔治数次询问进展，我知道自己再也不能拖延了。最后，我屏住呼吸，拨通了第一家公司的电话。电话接通了，我努力把“故事”编得逼真：我的假名、我的假公司以及随附的联系信息。终于，我听到了对方的声音。我汗流浃背，惊慌失措地挂断了电话。正当的商业活动不应该如此煎熬——我的个人信念占了上风。

我安排了一次约会，和我试图打电话的那家竞争对手公司的一位前顾问见面。结果，她能够在不违背保密协议的前提下，提供最新相关数据，那正是我所需要的。根据我在内部的访谈以及网络调研，我很快草拟了一份有关该公司的报告。带着这些可以交差的报告以及坚定的信念，我走向乔治的办公室。

我向他坦言，我不愿意用假冒的身份致电竞争对手。不管这是不是墨西哥公认的惯例，我都不认为这是一家跨国咨询公司该干的事情。我认同商业情报在生产、定价和推广的过程中起着举足轻重的作用，所以我提议用我的方法，即利用网络工具及我们的同事来获取尽可能多的正当数据。

尽管乔治在一开始对我的不合作有点失望，但他看重我的坦诚，也认识到自己的计划存在着潜在风险。他同意按照我的替代方案去办。这一事件不仅没有伤害我们的关系，还加强了我们之间的信任和尊重。他知道，我办事他可以放心，但他同时也知道，我会坚持我的原则。

33
诚实的界限

I was one of two consultants who conducted an independent assessment for a major financial services company. We were sponsored by its IT organization to assess the alignment of IT services to the various divisions and geographic locations of the business. During our assessment, we met with fifty of the top business leaders across four countries, including the CFO and CIO. We solicited their ideas for improvement and performed a statistical analysis of the results. When we shared the analysis with IT leadership, they asked us to remove some of the findings that reflected poorly upon their management practices before we reported the results to the business leaders.

Our dilemma was whether to report our independent findings to the business leaders against the wishes of IT leadership (who included our project sponsor) or to heed their request and dilute the findings. On the one hand, we reported to our project sponsor who paid our consulting fees and was our main contact at the company. On the other hand, we risked jeopardizing our credibility with the business leaders who had shared politically risky examples with us because they viewed the "independent" assessment as a vehicle for bringing about meaningful changes in the organization.

In order to address this dilemma, my colleague and I met to consider our options. Our reflection yielded one conclusion with two potential solutions. We concluded that all parties included in the assessment deserved to know the true findings of our study. As a result, we needed to either convince our sponsor that it was in his best interests to share the complete findings or find a way to show the limitations of the report's independence without alienating him.

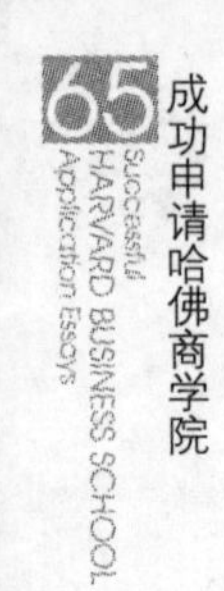

Ultimately, both solutions were necessary. During meetings with our sponsor, we pointed out that the business leaders would clearly identify the withholdings, which would compromise IT's credibility. We also noted that omitting results would contradict the assessment's goal of bringing about constructive changes. Our sponsor accepted the validity of our arguments and reduced the number of omissions. However, since full disclosure was not an option for the IT organization, we also worked collaboratively with our sponsor to include a section in the presentation about the process used to conduct the assessment that clearly identified the input that IT leadership had to the results. This approach was ultimately satisfactory to IT leadership. It also provided the necessary flag to alert the business leaders to the withholdings from our final presentation.

点评

本文讲述了一个许多顾问经常会面对的困境：要在评估中保持诚实，但不要太诚实，从而损害自己公司的利益（很可能还会影响奖金）。文章清晰地指出了问题所在，道出可行的解决办法，写得很有力量。结构清晰有序，即使不懂咨询业，也能明白申请人面临的困境。这一点很重要。不管你打算写什么，都应该假设读者对你的公司或行业知之甚少。

申请人提出的解决方案表明他非常成熟。他至少保留了一些关键信息，同时也清楚地指出，最终的演示受到了 IT 部门的影响。申请人认真负责，值得信任。他清楚谁给他付工资（客户），但同时也非常重视公司的声誉。结果虽然有妥协，但似乎皆大欢喜。也许，申请人有必要写一下故事的最终结局。比如，IT 部门是否按照建议完成了改革，或者咨询公司是否接到另外的项目？这些细节并非必不可少，但是可以让读者更好地了解事情如何收尾，以及客户是否受益于申请人的解决方案等。

【参考译文】

我曾是一位为一家庞大的金融服务公司作独立评估的咨询顾问。我们受该公司的 IT 总部资助，来评估公司各部门、各地分公司的 IT 服务。评估过程中，我们会见了来自 4 个国家 50 名公司的高层管理者，包括 CFO 和 CIO。我们向他们征求改进意见，然后对结果进行了统计分析。但在跟 IT 机构领导分享我们的分析结果时，对方要求我们在向该公司高层汇报之前，删除那些反映他们管理不当的调查结果。

我们陷入了困境。是应该违背 IT 部门领导（他是我们的项目资助人之一）的要求，向公司高层提供独立的调查结果？还是听从 IT 部门领导的要求，淡化那些结果的影响？一方面，我们向项目资助人汇报，由他们支付咨询费用，同时，他们也是我们在这家公司的主要联系人；另一方面，我们有可能在该公司高层管理人的心中信誉扫地。后者曾和我们分享行政风险案例，因为公司把这次“独立”评估当作工具，希望在组织内部引发有意义的变革。

为了解决问题，我和同事碰了个头，讨论对策。经过考虑，我们提出了两个可行的解决方案。我们认为，评估涉及的每一方都有权知道真实的分析结果。因此，要么我们说服资助人，公布完整的分析结果能使他的利益最大化；要么我们想办法，说明这份报告在独立性上作出了妥协，同时又不得罪 IT 部门的领导。

最终，两种解决方案都用上了。与资助人开会时，我们指出公司管理者会清楚地看到代扣所得税项，这将损害 IT 部门的信誉。同时指出，如果删除这部分结果，就违背了评估的初衷——带给部门建设性的变革。资助人接受了我们的理由，减少删除的内容。然而，既然 IT 部门不同意完全披露实情，我们还协同资助人，在演示时添加了一块内容，介绍评估的进行过程，指明 IT 部门的管理者对这份结果的影响。这个做法基本上令 IT 部门的管理者满意。在我们的最终演示上也提供了必要的标志，提醒公司管理者关注所得税代扣事项。

34
辞退还是留下?

It was a McKinsey project deep in the provinces of Russia. I had five client team members to manage. The team's initial ability to contribute was rather low as it often happens on out-of-town projects, but four team members caught up relatively quickly while one was constantly underperforming.

The obvious solution was to replace the underperforming team member. Project schedules are typically so tight that all team members should be strong performers. But this case was not so straightforward. The project got high visibility among the client's top managers. To replace the team member would have meant severe consequences for his career, not to say the end of it. On the other hand, my decision to keep him on the team, of course, would have resulted in increased workloads for other team members and especially for me.

First of all I tried to understand whether lack of skill or will was the reason for his underperformance, and when I realized he tried hard I decided to keep him on the team investing time in his development. At first I needed to help him gain back the respect of other team members. The latter figured out relatively quickly that the guy was delivering work of lower quality than they were and began to pick on him. The measures I took ranged from the direct interruption of the jokes to the demonstration of my own respect for him through asking his opinion before asking any of the others—listening attentively to what he had to say. Of course, these measures would not have had any success if they had not been supported by real improvements in the quality of his work. So, when the other team members were gone we were spending a couple of hours together discussing what he did well, what he could have done better, and what and how tasks should be done tomorrow. Gradually, the guy began to perform almost on par with the other team members.

I am still not sure it was the right decision. As I mentioned, the key decision-making factor for me was the team member's willingness to work hard to improve his performance. Someone else might argue that I would have added more value by focusing on developing top performers. I guess that is what a dilemma is about—there is no right or wrong decision, each person makes his own choice.

点评

申请人面临着一个艰难的决定：留下一个表现不佳的队员，但可能拖累项目；还是辞退他，后者可能导致他的饭碗被砸。在申请人看来，决策的关键是这位队员在努力提高。从这里，我们知道了申请人评价他人的方式，并且看到他要帮助队员走回正轨的决心。我们难以不同情这位努力奋斗的队员，也难以不赞赏申请人“收容”他的行为。我们把申请人看作一位良师：他不仅愿意给人第二次机会，还在他人面前维护这个人，即使这么做会危害他作为项目团队领导的立场。这些都是令人钦佩的品质。

本篇 Essay 的关键在于申请人怀疑他做的决策是否正确。他承认他不确定自己是不是做对了，并解释了他人对这事的看法会有怎样的不同。无论从哪个方面来看，最后一段都是最有意思、最精彩的。如果说本文还有什么地方可以提高的话，那就是可以加入更多正反两方面的讨论意见：是把精力放在业绩不好的人身上，还是培养潜在的明星工作人员。他还可以讨论一下挽救一位同事的职业生涯的价值，以及他的团队对客户的责任。就文章本身而言，它已经算得上是一篇佳作了，但申请人可以略微偏重于困境本身，而不是他如何帮助了一位奋斗的同事。

【参考译文】

这是麦肯锡咨询公司在俄罗斯内地省份的一个项目，我手下有 5 名客户团

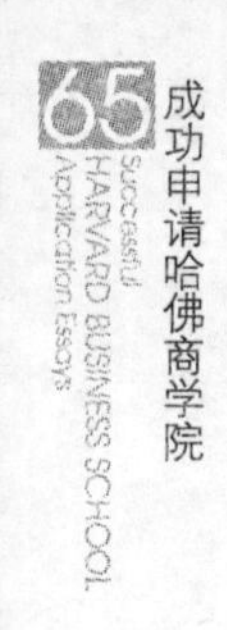

队成员需要管理。正如通常的出差项目一样，团队起初的工作能力相当差，不过，其中 4 位队员很快就进入了状态，只有一位队员一直表现不佳。

最容易的解决方案当然是换掉这位不称职的队员。项目进度一如既往的紧张，团队中的每位成员都应该是得力干将，但这个案子并不那么简单。客户的高级经理都盯着这个项目，换掉这位队员即使不会导致他职业生涯的终结，也会使其受到严重打击。当然，从另一方面来说，我若决定留下他，就必然会给其他队员，特别是我自己，增加工作量。

首先，我设法了解他表现不佳的原因——是缺乏技巧，还是缺乏意愿？当我意识到他已经非常努力了之后，我决定留下他，并花时间培养他。第一步，我需要帮助他重新获得其他队员的尊重。那些队员很快就看出这个家伙的工作质量不如他们，于是就开始挑他的刺了。我采取的措施有：直接打断他们的讥讽、在询问别人之前先征求他的意见以表示我对他的尊重，以及在他说话时认真倾听等。当然，这些措施若没有他的工作进步作支撑也没有用。所以，当其他队员下班后，我们花几个小时在一起谈论他做得好的地方、有待提高的地方、明天要完成的任务以及如何完成等。渐渐地，这位队员开始和其他人干得差不多了。

我仍然不太确定我做的决定对不对。如我之前提到的，影响我当时作决策的关键因素，是这位队员愿意付出努力提高自己的工作表现。别人或许会质疑说，如果我把精力放在培养优秀队员上，我会创造更多的价值。我猜，这就是所谓的进退两难的困境——决策没有对错，每个人都有自己的选择。

35
与习俗相悖时，如何坚持自我

In a country where "gifts" are common, and every speedily obtained official form implies one, existence is simply the partial resolution of one ethical dilemma after another.

Recently, my driver's license expired and I had to renew it. Since mail orders for such routine matters do not exist, I made my way to the DMV on a day when I should have been at headquarters lobbying for a government permit. Unless one slips a note (worth about $2) to one of the young cadets, the wait is endless. If I choose to commit a small felony, I can leave in ten minutes. I refuse to pay such "gifts," so I waited, and five hours later, I left the DMV.

Paradoxically, such "gifts" are never considered bribes in my country. The reason is simple; a young government official's salary does not exceed $20 per month, so any "side" money is considered a contribution or a "gift." The personal example above is an everyday issue applicable to many government dealings.

Back at the office, the scene was different, but the situation was identical. My company, a pioneer resort owner, was building the first five-star hotel in a particular area. We were waiting for the last of a series of approvals and documents to release imported equipment from customs. Seven government permits were required, and six were on my desk. The city's local council, inexperienced in such business deals, delayed this essential final document. This would lead to unbudgeted expenses, and a long setback would hurt the financial viability of the project. The threat was clear. I knew what was required: send a carrier with a small fee of less than $100. With this incentive, I could release the goods, and not delay the project. I said "no" anyway.

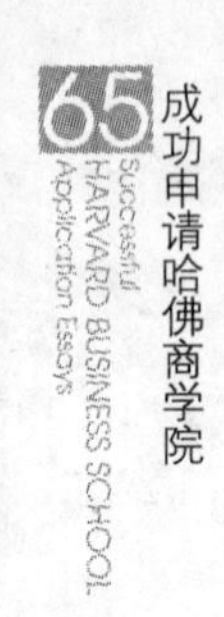

I explained my reasons to my boss who was already very anxious about the delay, and to my satisfaction, he complimented me. I retained a sense of freedom and moral integrity.

I continually discourage employees to pay petty "donations" to speed up their paperwork and impress their bosses. I would rather lose an entire project than damage the moral image of my country. Sometimes, the adherence to protocol can result in huge losses, but it is hardly comparable to forfeiting your own reputation and moral values.

点评

本文讲述的，是当申请人的价值观与习俗和常识相悖时如何坚持自我。第一段用一句话有效地阐明了问题的本质：困境很普遍，每天都在经受考验。文中的具体事例有助于了解问题涉及的范围。申请人一直受到大大小小的考验，但是信念让他每次都占上风。

申请人没有把他的道德行为局限于个人的选择，而是在努力维护民族"道德形象"，本文因此脱颖而出。鉴于这样的利害关系，浪费几小时排队或是失掉一个利润丰厚的合同显然都只是小代价。由此，申请人不仅传达了他对正确事物的执着，还表现出了他极强的公民意识和责任感。

【参考译文】

在这个国家，"收礼"是司空见惯的现象，每份官方文件要想得到迅速处理，都会暗示你送"礼物"，于是生活就是不断解决接踵而来的道德困境。

最近我的驾照到期，需要更新。那天我本该在总部游说一项政府批文，但由于这类日常事务不接受邮递处理，我只好亲自去一趟机动车管理局。除非塞张票子(约2美元)给一位年轻警卫,不然你就慢慢等吧。如果我选择犯点小罪，10分钟后就可以离开，但是我拒不送"礼"，于是我就等着，5小时后才离开机动车管理局。

令人纠结的是，在这个国家没人认为“送礼”是贿赂。原因很简单：一位年轻的政府官员每月工资不超过20美元，因此“副收入”被认为是一种捐助或者是“礼物”。上面提到的亲身经历就是例行程序，在处理许多政府事务时都会遇到。

回到办公室，场景虽然变了，但是情况一模一样。我的公司是一家经营度假村的领头企业，正在某一带建造首家五星级酒店。我们在等待进口设备所需的一系列批文中的最后一份。我一共需要7份政府许可，而我的办公桌上已有6份。当地的市政委员会对这种商业交易经验不足，耽误了最后一份重要文件。再等就要产生额外费用了，若是耽搁过久还会危及该项目的财务可行性，可能造成的危害显而易见。我知道，要做的就是寄去不到100美元的小费。有了这点“小意思”，货物就可以清关，工程也不会延误。但无论如何，我说了“不”。我跟老板解释了原因，他已经为此事焦急万分了。让我欣慰的是，老板赞扬了我，我维护了自由意志和诚实品质。

我不断劝告员工不要为了让文件加速处理、取悦老板而“捐小钱”。我宁愿丢掉整个项目，也不愿损害道德形象。有时候，坚持原则可能造成巨大的损失，但与丧失自己的声誉和道德观相比，不值一提。

36
勇于打破机构常规

I was working with a micro-finance institution that a U.S.-based Christian organization dedicated to development and relief work— helped establish in Kosovo. The organization in Kosovo is sustainable and financially independent, but its continuing legal affiliation with the U.S. organization makes it unclear whether its operations are, or should be, truly autonomous.

While the U.S. organization hires its employees exclusively from the Christian community, the group in Kosovo is not restricted by this requirement. I discovered, however, that the organization's hiring practices—relying on referrals from senior Christian staff—gave preferential treatment to members of the Christian community. It was unclear whether this preferential treatment in hiring was intentional, or whether it was even unethical. A private organization certainly had the right to hire whom it wished, did it not?

I felt uneasy in this ethical middle ground. Three main issues bothered me. First: These hiring practices went against our stated mission of promoting reconciliation between the Albanian and Serbian peoples, who have historically been divided along ethnic, linguistic, and religious lines. Second: Because we receive funds from donors, I felt we had an ethical obligation to use those funds (and tailor our practices) in accordance with the policies of the donor organizations. Preferential hiring based on religion ran contrary to the policies of a number of these donor organizations. Third: There appeared to be no set policy or standard within our own organization regarding hiring. Personnel and other policy matters seemed to change with the humor of each new director.

It was a difficult issue to broach with the director, not only because of its sensitivity, but also because I sensed that he might be using our paper affiliation with our parent organization to push his own religious agenda. I used our current search for a new loan officer as a starting point for a discussion of hiring practices. We had thus far interviewed only two, poorly qualified candidates—both employee referrals, and both from the Christian community. I expressed to him my concern about our limited applicant pool and suggested that all positions henceforth be advertised publicly in order to attract the most-qualified candidates and make the hiring process more transparent and equitable. He agreed. The following day I submitted the loan officer job description to the local newspaper. The response has been tremendous.

点评

这是一篇优秀的范文，申请人用一个微妙的道德困境展示了他身上多个值得称赞的性格特征。一开始，申请人甚至都不确定这样的招聘是否存在问题。他迫使自己冷静地检视形势，由此显示了他强烈的道德感。他一丝不苟地进行分析证明，即使面对容易引起情绪冲动的事情，他都能保持客观。他决定采取具体步骤来解决问题，而不是直接找领导探讨，这体现了他的政治手腕。申请人表明，他能够辨别、分析和解决道德上的问题，而且没有引发一场具有潜在破坏性的冲突。他强烈的道德感和办事能力在这里也一览无余。

故事发生在科索沃，这一点很有趣，也使本文脱颖而出，但它并不会自动形成一个道德困境。如果申请人面临的是企业背景下的类似问题，并同样具体地描述他的选择和行动，Essay 也一样会成功。

【参考译文】

当时，我在一家小型金融机构工作，它隶属于美国基督教组织，致力于发展和救济工作——在科索沃帮助重建。科索沃的该组织自给自足、财政独立，但它一直在法律上从属于美国组织，因此分不清它的运作究竟是否真的自治，或者说应该实现自治。

虽然美国机构只雇用基督徒，但科索沃团队则无此限制。然而，我发现，由于科索沃组织的招聘惯例依赖资深基督徒员工的推荐，所以会优待基督徒。很难说这种招聘时的优待是有目的性的，或者是不道德的。一个私人机构当然有权雇用它想要的人，不是吗？

我为自己处于这样的道德中间地带感到很不安。有三大问题困扰着我。第一，这样的招聘惯例违背了我们的使命，即促进阿尔巴尼亚人和塞尔维亚人和解，他们自古就在种族、语言、宗教问题上有分歧；第二，由于我们的财务来源是捐款，我觉得我们有义务按捐赠组织的方针使用善款（以及安排我们的工作），而基于宗教信仰的招聘偏好有违许多捐赠方的方针；第三，在我们组织内部，似乎并没有特定的招聘政策和标准，员工政策似乎是随着每一任新主管的心情而定的。

向主管提出这个问题很困难，不仅是因为事情本身的敏感性，也因为我感觉到他可能会用我们与上级机构的正式从属关系来推行他自己的宗教安排。我利用我们当时在寻找一位新的信贷员的机会开启了对招聘惯例的讨论。我们那时只面试了两位不合格的应聘者，而且两位应聘者都是由雇员推荐的，两位都是基督徒。我向主管表达了我对应聘者有限的担忧，建议以后所有工作岗位都公开登广告以吸引最合格的应聘者，也使招聘过程更透明、更公平。他同意了。第二天，我向当地报纸提交了信贷员一职的招聘启事，反响极大。

37
援助赌徒母亲的内心挣扎

Is it ever appropriate to say "no" to your mother when she needs financial assistance? While I was growing up, this was not a concept I could ever fathom. My mother is a hardworking woman. No job has ever been beneath her when it came to supporting the family—whether it was loading luggage on airplanes or lifting packages at a shipping company. My mother was the infallible beacon of hard work, my superstar in a single parent household. Unfortunately, certain situations over the past three years have created an ethical dilemma in our relationship.

My love for my mother compelled me to eagerly enter the workforce in order to support her with supplemental income. However, her financial situation has deteriorated significantly over the past few years due to efforts to make up for shortfalls in her income by gambling at casinos. Her reliance on legal gambling has developed into borderline addiction. Due to inopportune losses, she has often turned to me for assistance in paying her rent and utility bills.

I tried to be supportive and encouraging by assisting her with creating a budget and getting her in touch with financial counselors. The situation has been emotionally difficult for me, as her requests for money have increased. While I consider myself to be financially responsible and disciplined, it is difficult for me to continue feeling comfortable supporting her behavior through passive measures. I often fear that my assistance may be more detrimental than helpful. As a resolution, I recently tried declining her continued requests for financial assistance. Of course, I cannot make such a decision without fierce internal conflict and in the end, I simply felt guilty for saying "no."

I have given her the money that she needed on every occasion. I do so because I realize that everything that I have attained in my career is in large part due to her unconditional love and support. Under normal circumstances, I would not hesitate to support her financially, but this situation is troubling because I am also the source of the family's long-term financial stability. Realistically, I must think in terms of my own future, as I have no one to turn to in case of a financial emergency of my own. While I have yet to discover a final resolution to this ongoing dilemma, what I have found is that while in some situations, I should say "no" to my mother, I have a moral obligation to provide her with a supportive network, just as she did for me when I was a child.

点评

申请人跟我们分享了一个私人问题。然而单单指出问题，这篇文章的意义肯定不够深刻。本文的说服力在于申请人详细描述了他如何作出最后的决定。多次尝试提高母亲的理财能力均以失败告终，表明他是如何不得不采取最后的极端措施的，其内心情绪的纠葛不言而喻。

从他对后果的深刻认识可以看出，不管申请人采取了什么行动，尽管内心有着激烈的冲突，但是他能够抽身而出，理性地考虑备选方案。他始终能够从长远着眼，这表明他异常成熟。因此，本文不仅讲述了一个令人同情的故事，也是申请人正直刚强的个性的表现。

【参考译文】

当母亲需要经济资助时，你能对她说“不”吗？即使年龄在一年一年地增长，这个问题我始终无法回答。母亲是一个吃苦耐劳的人，为了养家糊口，她什么工作都做过——无论是在机场装行李，还是到运输公司打包裹。母亲曾经犹如一座值得信赖的灯塔一般，辛勤劳作，昼夜不息，是这个单亲家庭里的超级明星。不幸的是，过去三年里的一些事情给我俩的关系造成了困扰。

爱母之情催促我早日工作，赚钱补贴家用。然而，由于母亲每逢入不敷出就靠去赌场赌博贴补家用，所以她的财务状况在过去几年内每况愈下。她对赌博的依赖已经到了上瘾的边缘，经常因为赌博输钱，求我帮她付房租和水电费。

我帮母亲制订财务预算，联系财务顾问，试图支持、鼓励她，但她要的钱越来越多，这让我在情感上备受煎熬。尽管我认为自己能够自力更生，花钱也算节制，但是要我继续爽快地无条件支持她实在太难了！我常常担心，这么做是在害她，而不是在帮她。最近，我下定决心拒绝她那些无休无止的要求。当然，我不可能不经历一番激烈的内心冲突。而且最终，我甚至对说“不”感到心怀内疚。

每次母亲管我要钱，我都如数给她。这么做是因为我知道，我从工作中得到的一切，很大程度上要感谢她无私的关爱和支持。正常情况下，我会毫不犹豫地资助她，但我还是这个家长期收入的稳定来源，这样的情形令人不安。现实情况是，我必须为自己的未来考虑，因为我若出现财务危机，没人可以求助。虽然我还没有找到应对目前这一困境的解决方法，但是我发现，虽然在某些情况下我应该拒绝母亲，但是从道义上讲，我仍然有责任给她提供一把保护伞，就像小时候她为我做的那样。

38
举报老师性骚扰

In high school, a teacher began writing me letters that became increasingly inappropriatc as the year passed. He had been my most intellectually engaging teacher, and I had chosen him as an independent-study advisor in my senior year. Most indiscretions occurred during these sessions. It took me time to acknowledge the situation, but eventually, I considered reporting him. Oddly, I feared for his job and worried even more for the well-being of his son, who was also a student at my school. Because Addington waived tuition for teachers' children, if this teacher were fired, his son, on top of his personal suffering, would have lost his seat. The situation was further complicated as his son, Joe, was my younger brother's friend. Though the letters disturbed me, having grown up in a supportive family and community, I was able to compartmentalize them as the misgivings of an unfulfilled man. Though I was torn about coming forward, I decided to protect Joe by remaining silent.

The events stayed with me through my first year in college, and by Thanksgiving, I realized that I had made the wrong decision. Not understanding the dilemma I had faced, I thought I had picked between defending myself and adversely altering the life of my brother's friend. In high school, I believed that I had acted selflessly to preserve Joe's adolescent experience. However, by not coming forward, I realized I had put other women attending Addington at risk. Yet, as Joe was still a student there, the dilemma I faced was between protecting other potential victims at Addington and preserving Joe's welfare.

I decided I had to speak to the headmaster. Walking into his office during Thanksgiving break, I still hoped to preserve Joe's remaining seven months. My plan was to speak with Mr. Smith about sexual harassment broadly at Addington. I told him that I did not want to reveal specific events, but that it was a widespread problem. As a solution, I volunteered to work with him to set community standards on sexual harassment. The goal would be to get every teacher to sign a contract agreeing to these standards and to communicate them throughout the school. Though Mr. Smith pushed for examples, I was able to convince him that the problem existed without revealing details. The sexual harassment community standards were instituted by February. Joe graduated Addington, and his father left the school shortly afterwards.

Note: All names, including the school name, have been changed to preserve confidentiality.

点评

申请人勇敢地分享了一段非常私人的经历。话题的严重性立刻使本篇 Essay 脱颖而出，令人过目难忘。然而，简单地分享一次受伤的往事是不够的，文中所传达的申请人的性格和个人价值的广度才是真正让本文脱颖而出的关键。

例如，在她升入大学之后，她仍想保护高中的其他女生，这显示出她具有极强的道德使命感，体现出她的选择不只是为了自己的生活，也是为了整个社会。大多数人大概会选择忘却不愉快的经历，可她不能明知有人身处危险而不作为。

此外，本文还可以看出申请人性格的另一面，即主动承认错误——这在容易冲动的道德困境中更是难能可贵。她认定“什么也不做”是错误的选择，表现出自己极强的正直感，尤其是对她自己而言。最后，她采取了行动，同时避免与当事人直接冲突，这证明了她在处理困难局面时的沉着冷静。

【参考译文】

上高中时，有位老师开始给我写信，而且一年过去了，信的内容越来越不像话。论学识，他是我最欣赏的老师，高三那年，我还选他作为我独立课题研究的导师，而最不像话的事情就发生在这个阶段。我花时间确认了情况，但最终，我考虑举报他。说来奇怪，我怕他丢了工作，更担心他的儿子会受牵连——他儿子也是我们学校的学生。因为阿丁顿学校为教师子女减免学费，所以，如果这位老师被解雇了，除了他个人受损外，他的儿子也可能会面临失学的问题。他儿子乔还是我弟弟的朋友，这就使情况更加复杂了。虽然这些信件让我烦恼，不过我从小生活在一个相互帮助的家庭和社区里，所以我能够把它们视为一位不能得到满足的男人的困惑。虽然我为是否投诉而纠结，但我最终还是决定为了保护乔而保持沉默。

这件事在我读完大学一年级之后仍然存在。直到感恩节，我意识到我之前的决定是错误的。由于我当时不理解自己面对的困境，误以为自己是在保护自己与破坏弟弟朋友的生活之间作选择。高中时，我相信我的无私行为保护了乔的青少年生活。然而，我意识到，由于我没有及时举报，使得这个问题转移到阿丁顿学校的其他女学生身上。尽管乔仍然是那里的学生，但我所面临的困境却变成了在保护阿丁顿学校其他可能的受害者与维护乔的福利之间作选择。

我决定去找校长谈谈。感恩节假期里，我走进了校长的办公室。我还是希望能让乔读完他剩下的7个月，因此我打算向史密斯先生笼统地说说阿丁顿学校内存在的性骚扰现象。我告诉他，我不想揭露具体的事件，但这确实是一个普遍存在的问题。我提出和他一起制订有关性骚扰的公共准则作为解决方案，目的是让每位教师签字同意这些准则，并在全校范围内传达。尽管史密斯先生要求我提供实例，但我还是在不披露细节的前提下说服了他，告诉他这个问题的确存在。有关性骚扰的公共准则在2月开始实施，而乔也从阿丁顿学校毕业了。随后不久，他的父亲也离开了学校。①

① 为了保密，本文所有人名、校名都用了化名。

THREE ACCOMPLISHMENTS

命题6

重要的成就

What are your three most substantial accomplishments, and why do you view them as such?

你最大的三项成就分别是什么？为什么这么认为？

解题思路

这可能是申请哈佛商学院时必做的 Essay 命题之一。其他 Essay 命题在每年都会有所不同，但这篇 Essay 命题总是能够看到。在这里，可以为其他作文已经讨论的主题补充事例，也可以表现自己的其他特质，而且是在其他作文里不明显的特质。

把这个命题当成是展示你三张快照的地方。尽管没有明确的规定，但是大多数申请人都会从生活中的三个不同方面选择成功事例，并用大约 200 字的篇幅来描述每项成就。许多作文都套用写作公式，即一项课外成就、一项学术成就、一项事业成就，但你并非必须遵守这个公式。

你可能担心自己的成就是否够分量。赢得奥运金牌够吗？从着火的大厦里救出一个小孩够吗？答案是肯定的，但并非每一位哈佛商学院的学生都有机会有如此壮举，实际上，有此类经历的人寥寥无几，关键是要解释清楚你认为这些成就重要的原因。下面的几篇经典 Essay 正阐释了这一点。

分享这些经历时，申请人经常难以决定到底哪些经历涉及太多个人隐私，哪些又太久远。正如下列范文所阐释的，可以切入的角度有很多，不必把话题局限在学习和工作之上。

点评人：胡玲（Ling Hu）

39
粉碎性骨折后的 4 个侧手翻

1

My most substantial accomplishment was my recovery from a motorcycle accident on September 9, 1996, my junior year at Tufts. On the way to Harvard Square, a drunk driver swerved in front of my oncoming motorcycle. My legs collided with the roof of her car, and I was catapulted through the air at over forty miles per hour, landing headfirst on the asphalt. I awoke from surgery eighteen hours later with four lacerated nerves and titanium rods securing my shattered femur, radius, ulna, and hand.

Following two weeks in the hospital, the orthopedic surgeon predicted I'd never have full use of my hand again, and suggested that I go to a special rehab clinic in California. "Rehab will fix my bones, but my brain will turn to mush," I thought. I phoned school the next day to find out which of my classes were wheelchair accessible. I spent the next semester wheeling through the Boston winter to physical therapy three times a day while studying astronomy and Russian.

It was the most painful, and challenging, time of my life. At graduation two years later, I was awarded Tufts's Ellen C. Myers Award for "outstanding scholarship in the face of adverse circumstances." The next day, I went back to Mass. General, and did four cartwheels across my doctor's office—never say never.

2

Next is the BroadbandCompass, a software program conceived in the basement of a nondescript building in a Denver-area business park. My five partners and I had only a dream, plus hand-me-down hardware and a few free ninety-day evaluation licenses for Web server software. We outlined the framework for our platform. Two years of strategy work at MediaOne Cable had convinced us it was time somebody made finding a broadband connection online as easy as finding a book on Amazon.com.

Funded with about a nickel over a million dollars, we labored for two years in that basement writing software code and convincing America's largest access providers, electronics retailers, and Web portals that our platform would change the way people looked for Internet access. We drudged through the Internet boom and the dot-com bust. But we made it. Today, our tool is leveraged by industry giants such as Office Depot, Gateway, Microsoft, CompUSA, Circuit City, and numerous others. I am proud to say I wrote Product Specification V.1.0 for the technology that's helped one in ten Internet users find a broadband connection.

3

I am proud of my music. I have been obsessed with entertaining large crowds ever since I first laid hands on a pair of turntables in high school. I began my career as a bilingual "turntablist" my senior year abroad at a nightclub called Taxman in Moscow. Since then, I have developed a repertoire that includes gigs in some of Europe's and America's largest nightclubs, including sellout crowds of more than two thousand people. I enjoy convincing critics that mixing records is an art form, not just aimless basement shenanigans. Following the abrupt demise of a nightclub venture in 1998 (see "failure" question for details), I founded Amazing Productions Inc., a mobile disc jockey service. Though entertaining has never been my full-time occupation, it has always been my full-time passion. My knack for technology gives Amazing Productions a competitive advantage in the Denver market, as our shows have become known for their array of high-tech marvels. These range from blends of musical media—including vinyl, CDs, and MP3s—to computer-driven acoustics, lasers, and special effects. We have operated profitably since Ql 99, and have since become a household name in the Denver DJ industry. Check us out at www.amazingdj.com.

点 评

本篇 Essay 不仅内容翔实，而且题材新颖，成功地敲开了哈佛商学院的大门。申请人用充满生气的文字，通过描写三个成就来展现自己活力四射的个性。紧张刺激的内容，加上丰富多彩的形容词以及动人心弦的描写，令读者着迷。

申请人能够通过 Essay 展示自我而非坐而论道，是一位令人难忘的候选人。4 个侧手翻穿过医生办公室，在展示他的文学修养之余，还展示了身体的灵活性。无论是面对悲惨经历，还是在商界打拼，申请人都是一副乐观、谦逊的态度，并将自己塑造成战士的形象。文中提及的学习天文学、俄语的经历，以及对编程和技术、音乐的狂热，可以看出申请人兴趣广泛。本篇 Essay 能够脱颖而出的原因是申请人鲜明的个性，让人想与之深入交往。这些都是制胜招式，在构思自己的文章时应该牢记。

【参考译文】

1

我在 1996 年 9 月 9 日遭遇了一起摩托车事故，能够从那次创伤中复原是我最大的成就。当时我在美国塔夫斯大学读大一。我骑着摩托车去哈佛广场，迎面驶来的一位醉酒司机突然转向，直直地冲我撞上来。我的两条腿撞在车顶上，整个人以每小时 65 千米的速度弹出去，头先落地，磕在沥青马路上。在进行了 18 个小时的手术后，我终于苏醒过来，但 4 根神经被撕裂，股骨、桡骨、尺骨和手均已粉碎性骨折，被安上了钛合金支架。

随后是两周的住院期，整形外科医生预言我的手将永远无法正常活动，建议我去加州一家康复中心治疗。我心想："康复中心可以治愈我的骨头，但我的脑子恐怕就要变成一团浆糊了。"于是，第二天，我打电话给学校，询问哪些课程有轮椅通道。那个学期，我在轮椅上度过了波士顿的冬天，一天三次物理治疗，同时学习天文学和俄语。

这是我一生中最艰难、痛苦的时间。两年后毕业时，我获得了塔夫斯大学的艾伦·迈尔斯奖，用以表彰"逆境下的杰出学术成就"。第二天，我回到马萨诸塞州总医院，做了 4 个侧手翻穿过我的主治医师的办公室——永不言败。

2

第二个成就是“宽带指南针”（Broadband Compass）软件，它由我和其他5个朋友一起，在丹佛地区商业园区一座不起眼的大楼的地下室研发而成。我们怀揣着梦想和几台二手机器、一些可以免费试用90天的网络服务器软件，勾勒出了“宽带指南针”这个平台的框架。在第一媒体有限公司（MediaOne Cable）战略部门两年的工作经历让我们确信时机已经成熟，我们可以让用户在网上寻找宽带连接点像在亚马逊网站上找书一样容易。

在仅有100多万美元初始资金的情况下，我们在地下室工作了两年。编写程序代码，游说美国最大的网络提供商、电器零售商和门户网站，让他们相信这个平台会改变人们连接互联网的方式。熬过了互联网繁荣时期，又熬过了网络泡沫破灭阶段，我们终于成功了。今天，诸如欧迪办公、Gateway公司、微软公司、CompUSA公司、电路城公司等行业巨头纷纷投资我们的软件。我感到非常荣幸，这套软件的产品规格说明书V.1.0是我亲手写的，有1/10的互联网用户用它找到了宽带连接。

3

我为自己的音乐成就感到自豪。自从读高中时第一次将手放在唱盘上，我就迷上了在众人面前打碟。我的音乐职业生涯始于大四时游学国外，在莫斯科一家名叫“税务大人”的夜总会做一名“双语唱盘手”。从那时起，我组编了一整套曲目，在包括欧洲和美国一些大型夜总会的演奏会上演出，其中有些场次聚集了2 000多人。我喜欢与批评家辩论，说服他们打碟是一种艺术形式，而不是毫无目的的玩耍。继1998年夜总会突然消亡之后，我成立了“奇迹制作公司”，专门提供移动DJ服务。虽然我从来不曾全职打碟，但它却一直是我心之所系。随着我们的节目成为丹佛市场的高科技成就系列，我的技术成了“奇迹制作公司”在当地的竞争优势。高科技成就包括由混合音乐媒介（黑胶唱片、光盘和MP3）到由电脑制作的音响效果、激光和特效。从1999年第一季度开始，我们就有了盈余，此后还成了丹佛DJ行业的知名品牌。欲了解更多信息，请登陆网站www.amazingdj.com。

40
为艾滋病预防教育募捐，受白宫接待

The three most substantial accomplishments in my life comprise an athletic, a personal, and a professional accomplishment. These accomplishments have rewarded me with confidence in myself and my abilities, because they proved to me that I was capable of successfully handling difficult challenges.

The first accomplishment was the Pedro Zamora National College Bike Tour. I was one of five college students who organized, arranged financing for, and completed a cross-country bicycle tour from Los Angeles to Boston. We spoke at twenty-seven colleges with the objective of raising awareness on college campuses about the threat that HIV poses to college students. In Washington, D.C., we were received at the White House by First Lady Hillary Clinton. Additionally, we raised over $50,000 from corporate sponsors for HIV prevention education. I consider the tour to be one of my most rewarding accomplishments in terms of the physical and organizational challenges as well as the thought that we might have encouraged someone to behave differently and thereby, potentially avoid contracting HIV. The trip also taught me how to push myself and my teammates to perform beyond our abilities as individuals.

The second accomplishment was living and working abroad for three and a half years. I knew that I wanted to travel the world and have a career in international business. I just did not know where to start or how to gain experience. I tried to obtain a job overseas while still in school but ran into the problem that I did not have any significant work experience. I almost decided to give up and wait until later in my career to work overseas. But, something in my mind pushed me to take the risk and go for it. After graduating from college, I traveled in Australia and Africa for three months. When I ran low on money, I went to London in search of a job.

Fortunately, I quickly found a job as an analyst for a firm based in Switzerland. I was soon transferred to the Swiss headquarters and then on to Chile. Over those three and a half years, I traveled to forty countries on six continents, gained significant international work experience, and learned a great deal about myself from exposure to new ideas and situations.

The third accomplishment results from a work experience. In June 1999, the company I worked for transferred me from Switzerland to Chile to conduct a survey of the Chilean market for a particular chemical used in the copper refining process. If the market proved to be attractive, the company planned to construct a $2 million local production facility. My role was to develop a business model including market size and price structure, production costs and a return on investment analysis to determine whether the plant would be successful or not.

I was somewhat daunted by the task, since a $2 million decision would be made based on my evaluation of the project. Over the course of six months, I met with the majority of our potential customers in order to produce a detailed market survey, found a suitable piece of property to locate the plant, worked with local engineering firms to develop plant construction costs, and produced a detailed production cost model based on market factors. After completing my analysis, I successfully recommended that the project not be pursued because of an unacceptably low return. This project offered me a significant level of responsibility, and I am pleased that I was able to meet such a tough professional challenge.

点评

申请人漂亮地将三个故事天衣无缝地串连在一起。他的文字色彩丰富、细节饱满，从而使他的成就栩栩如生，也使本篇 Essay 超越了一纸空谈，向读者证实了他的成就。正如这部分的许多经典 Essay，关键是说服读者，让读者相信你所做的对你来说很重要，而并非论述成就本身的重要性。这一点看似微妙，却值得牢记。在一笔 500 万美元的订单中，担任一个人微言轻的角色，除了说明这是笔大买卖之外，其意义远不如本篇 Essay 的申请人描写的那样：在一个相对小的项目中发挥举足轻重的影响。华而不实的数据比不上你的所作所为，也比不上你吸取的经验教训。总免不了有其他人参与了更大的生意，所以不要试图以单纯的金额大小取胜。

申请人勇气可嘉、富有好奇心，是你在长途飞行中希望遇到的邻座聊伴。达到这个效果的关键是本篇 Essay 的语调：平易近人、实事求是、毫不傲慢（傲慢永远是在描写成就时容易进入的误区）。

【参考译文】

我一生中最大的成就有三项，分别是一项体育方面的成就、一项个人生活方面的成就，以及一项职业方面的成就。这些成就给了我无比的信心，让我相信自己、相信自己的能力，因为它们向我证实了，我能够成功地处理艰难的挑战。

第一项成就是彼得罗·扎莫拉国立大学自行车骑行。由 5 位大学生组织并为此次活动筹款，还完成了一次从洛杉矶到波士顿的横穿全国的自行车骑行，而我就是其中之一。我们在 27 所大学演讲，旨在提高大学校园对艾滋病危害的认识。在华盛顿时，第一夫人希拉里·克林顿在白宫接见了我们。另外，我们还从企业赞助商那里，为艾滋病预防教育募集到 5 万多美元。我认为这次骑行是我最有价值的成就之一，因为我不仅在体能和组织能力上经受了挑战，我们甚至改变了某些人的行为，从而避免了感染艾滋病的潜在威胁。这次骑行还教会我如何鞭策自己和队员突破个人极限，超水平发挥。

第二项成就是在海外生活、工作了三年半。我知道自己想要环游世界，在跨国企业谋职，只是不知道从哪里开始，不知道如何累积经验。我还在读书的时候，曾想去海外工作，当时遇到的障碍就是我的工作经验不够。我几乎要放弃了，准备等工作一段时间后再去海外发展。但是，我脑海中有一个声音催促着我去冒险、去追寻。大学毕业后，我去澳大利亚和非洲旅行了三个月。囊中羞涩时，我又前往伦敦寻找工作。幸运的是，我很快在一家总部设在瑞士的公司找到了一份分析师的工作。不久，我就被调往瑞士总部，后来又去了智利。在那三年半的时间里，我去过 6 大洲共 40 个国家，获得了宝贵的国际工作经验，接触的新观点和新环境让我对自己的认识更深刻。

第三项成就来自于一次工作经历。1999 年 6 月，我所在的公司把我从瑞士

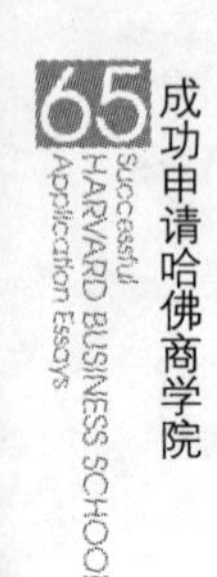

调去智利，目的是调查一种用于炼铜的特殊化学品在智利市场上的销售情况。如果市场销路看好，公司打算在当地投资 200 万美元建设生产线。我的任务是设计一个商业模型来判断工厂能否成功，模型包括市场规模、价格结构、生产成本及投资收益分析。

不知为何，面对这个任务，我有点胆怯。一个涉及金额 200 万美元的决定就全看我对这个项目的评估了！在那 6 个月的时间里，我与大多数潜在客户一一见面以进行周密的市场调查；找到了一处适合建造工厂的地产；与当地工程公司一起测算出了工厂建造费用；还设计了一个综合各种市场因素的详细的生产成本模型。分析报告完成后，发现回报太低，我成功地向公司建议放弃该项目。这个项目赋予我重大的责任感，我为自己能够胜任如此艰巨的职业挑战而感到自豪。

41
救护车司机的爱与痛

Four years after I had initially set myself the goal, I succeeded in winning the National Mathematics Competition in Germany. Seeing prolonged struggle turn into eventual success makes this one of my most valuable achievements. It helped me form an "it can be done" attitude that has stayed with me ever since. I first learned of the competition during a summer program in 1990 where I met some former finalists. The following year, when I was on exchange in the U.S., I had the competition materials sent over from Germany. I made it though the first two rounds to become one of seventy finalists invited to a weekend where the five national winners would be chosen. I wasn't one of them. The following year I again advanced to the finals only to fail at the last test. I continued to work on my skills and when I made it to the finals for the third time in a row, I knew it was my last chance. I had to survive a grilling by university professors on an unknown topic, but this time I could solve every problem. Walking out of the interview I knew I had won. Three days later the letter arrived. It was a dream come true.

An accomplishment of a different kind is my work as an ambulance driver, which I chose as an alternative to military service. After gaining a qualification as a paramedic I started to man ambulances in my hometown near Düsseldorf. I worked both in supervised medical transports between hospitals and in emergency situations. My strongest memory is of the death of a child when we hit a traffic jam and could not make it to the hospital in time. I was in the back of the car with the boy and his mother. I never felt more helpless in my life. But there are also many happy memories, of the people whom we succeeded in helping during emergencies and of the many grateful patients on our regular transport services. During the fifteen months on the ambulances I matured tremendously. I learned to take on responsibility for other people when they needed me the most. I dealt with extreme pressure and human tragedy. These were enormous challenges to overcome. But every day I was also able to experience how gratifying helping others can be. I view my time on the ambulances as an achievement because I was able to learn and grow, but more importantly for the help we were able to provide to the patients and the community.

My third achievement is having a significant impact on the trading strategies of the currency options group at Goldman Sachs. I began developing my own pricing spreadsheets soon after I joined the group. Being in the privileged position of combining a strong mathematical background with the practical grasp of the market that our "rocket scientist" developers lacked, I was able to arrive at several innovations. Whilst some enthusiastically supported my work (it would not have been possible otherwise), I encountered opposition from senior members of the group who lacked the younger traders' quantitative background and feared that eventually innovation would undermine their power base. I persevered, using my trading portfolio as a trial ground. Eventually, the better ideas prevailed and my interpolation now forms the basis of the strategy that group uses to identify value in the market. I am proud of having had the spirit and ability to innovate our strategies, but it is the strength to carry on in the face of adversity that makes this my biggest professional achievement to date.

点评

你没必要使自己看上去像个大英雄，别掉进这个陷阱。如果你能把自己描述成英雄，那最好，但是这样的文章既不现实也没必要。本文申请人坦承自己的弱点，感谢那些帮助他实现目标的人，这显示了他的成熟和谦逊，这样的个性使他引人注目。

申请人讲述了他如何面对逆境。对他来说，成就是不断战胜失败和挫折的过程：如果他第一次参加数学竞赛就成功了，如果他挽救了每个救护车的病人，那么他的故事就不可能有如此大的影响力。可他也并没长篇大论地讲述这些挫折，相反，他把重点放在如何解决问题上。读完本文之后，你记住的是申请人“凡事皆可能”的态度。

申请人选择按时间顺序讲述他的三个成就，第一个故事与后两个故事前后呼应，效果很好。再次提醒，连贯性并非强制要求，不过这为本文的整体效果增色不少。

【参考译文】

离最初制订目标过去了4年，我终于成功地赢得德国国家级数学竞赛。长期的努力终获成功，它成为我最宝贵的成就之一，它使我相信“凡事皆可能”。自那以后，这种态度伴随我至今。我第一次听说这个比赛是在1990年我参加的一个暑期项目里，我还见到了前几届的决赛入围选手。次年我在美国做交换学生，其间，我将竞赛所需的准备材料从德国寄了过来。我通过了最初两轮筛选，成为70名决赛选手之一，可以参加周末的比赛，角逐全国五强。不幸的是，我没能进军五强。第二年我再接再厉，再次晋级决赛，只是没有闯过最后一关。我继续努力，在连续三次挺进决赛后，我知道这是我最后的机会。一群大学教授就一个事先没有准备的话题拷问我，但是这次，每个问题我都应答自如。走出面试的房间，我知道我赢了。三天后，信来了。梦想终于成真了。

第二个成就是在当救护车司机和服兵役二选一时，我选择当一名救护车司机。在拿到急救资格后，我便开始在家乡（靠近杜塞尔多夫）开救护车。我不仅负责在医疗监护下的转院运送，也负责运送急救病人。我印象最深的一次是，因为塞车，我没能及时把一个孩子送到医院。我就和那个男孩，还有他妈妈一起坐在救护车的后部。我的一生中从未感到过如此无助。当然，也有许多美好的回忆。例如那些我们及时送到的急救病人，还有许多常规转院运输遇到的病人，他们对我千恩万谢。在救护车上的15个月让我成熟了很多。我学会了在别人最需要我的时候分担他们的责任；学会了排解极端压力，面对人间悲剧，这些都是需要超越的艰难阻碍。但是，每一天，我依然能从帮助别人的过程中体会到满足感。因为能够从中学习并且成长，我认为救护车上的工作经历算是一项成就。更重要的是，我们能够为病人以及社会提供帮助。

我的第三个成就，是我大大改变了高盛货币期权组的交易策略。加入货币

期权组不久，我就开始设计自己的定价试算表。我既有扎实的数学背景，又对市场现状认识深刻（这点是那些天才设计人员所缺乏的），这样的优势使我设计出了不少创新的计算方式。虽然有些同事热情支持我的工作（如果没有他们的支持，这些创新将不可能成功），但是我也遭到了团队里资深成员的反对，他们没有年轻交易员的数学背景，却担心别人的创新最终会削弱他们的权力基础。我坚持用我的交易组合作为测试平台。最终，更好的计算方式占了上风。现在，我的内推法变成了小组用来确定市场价值的交易策略基础。我为拥有改善交易策略的精神和能力而自豪，但是面对别人的反对，坚持己见的勇气才使这件事称得上是我迄今为止最伟大的职业成就。

42
培养企业的社会责任意识

I wrote my first short story at eight. It was five pages long and truly awful. But it was too late; I loved writing. Since then I have written innumerable stories and four feature-film screenplays.

The Big Deal was my fourth script, set in the world of high finance. It's a comedy, based on the concept of floating the UK on the stock exchange; its satirical backbone is from my own firsthand corporate experience.

Why is this an accomplishment? It's my best writing to date. It's been short-listed for a European Union development fund. It's been optioned by a production company. It's currently at a global talent agency as a showcase script.

Screenwriting is the most collaborative writing medium, with a strong team element (from producers to editors and directors) and I approach it with no less rigor or commitment than my job; neither are they mutually exclusive, as I work in consulting to media companies. Every time I write, it's a new challenge, finding solutions to creative problems. I pour my heart and energies into it. I have trekked the Himalayas and the Andes, but I'm most proud of my little mountain of scripts. It's my character on a page.

Two years ago, I worked on the pan-European launch of Sony's next-generation console, PlayStation 2. Using statistical programs, I crafted customer segmentations and designed marketing campaigns, capitalizing on Accenture's technological solutions. Additionally, I helped develop a retail strategy to ensure maximum customer data-capture.

As a strategy consultant, it is rare to see a project from conception to implementation. However, on this job, I worked for months before the launch and witnessed the product's phenomenal success. This was the largest-ever consumer electronics launch in Europe, and in the UK alone, one in five households has a PlayStation.

After two years of working as a consultant at Accenture, this was the first time I had been given real responsibility to lead a work-stream. Presenting my work to senior executives at Sony, my contribution was met with huge client satisfaction and my company rewarded me with a promotion. Additionally, the industry captivated me as an area that blends technology with artistry and commerce. For the first time I experienced the fusion of creativity and enterprise. Media and entertainment; I'd found my industry.

This year, I traveled to a Bosnian orphanage on charitable leave. Inspired by the book *Welcome to Sarajevo*, I decided to travel there to see those left behind. I found a crumbling institution, packed with children, some mentally and physically abused. The building had been shelled during the war and some had seen their parents murdered. But I was inspired by the love and commitment of the charity's staff. They coped as best they could, surviving on imagination and resilience. I interviewed them, took photographs and promised to help them.

Back home, I worked with the charity to draft a proposal to Accenture, structuring the messages to ensure maximum impact within my organization, and I lobbied key executives. We secured $40,000. I have since been invited by the charity to Rwanda and Sierra Leone.

I take great pride in this achievement. I made the journey just before my father died. As British ambassador, he had dedicated his life to bringing security to strangers around the world. He didn't always understand my work as a consultant; however, after my trip I knew he was so proud. He saw I had used the resources available to me to realize change.

This experience has grown my desire to build a lasting partnership between the charity and Accenture, fostering a culture of corporate responsibility.

点评

一个小男孩写着歪歪扭扭的字，双脚从高脚凳上垂下，来回晃动着……申请人通过描绘这样一幅景象抓住了读者。申请人对自己作品的评价诚实而有趣(那部小说当然文法不通——他才8岁呢!),也是一种调节气氛的好方法。你能看出,他并没有拿自己太当回事。

文章的内容以及申请人的文采使得本文毫不呆板。申请人避免老生常谈,同时传达了他对写作的热情:“我曾登过喜马拉雅山和安第斯山,但最引以为傲的还是那堆积成山的手稿。”在撰写成就故事时,他预料到读者会有这样的疑问:“为什么去读商科学校,而不去成为一名作家?”申请人通过指出商科与写作之间关键的一个相似点,即两者都是在创造性地解决问题,回答了读者的疑问。这篇文章是将三个成就故事融入同一个主题的又一个典范。申请人在这一点上完成得非常出色,三个故事各有不同但又很相似,很快,一个更加高大的人物形象便展现在了我们面前。

【参考译文】

8岁那年,我完成了自己第一部短篇小说。只有5页,而且故事糟透了。可惜还是太晚了,我已经爱上了写作。自那以后,我写了数不清的小说和4部剧情电影的剧本。

《大买卖》是我的第4个剧本,故事背景设定在金融界高层。这是一部喜剧,基本剧情是“英国”在证券交易所上市流通,这充满讥讽意味的内容正来源于我在企业的亲身经历。

为什么这算一项成就呢?因为这是迄今为止我写得最好的作品。它曾进入欧盟发展基金候选名单,也曾被一家制片公司列为选择对象。目前,它作为手稿正在一家全球猎头公司中展出。

剧本创造是最体现协作精神的一种媒介形式,需要很强的团队意识(从制片人到编辑和导演),而我对待它的严谨态度绝不比本职工作少一分一毫,何况两者并非全然无关,因为我的工作就是为媒体公司提供咨询服务。每一次动笔都是一次新的挑战——为创造性问题寻找解决方法。我对它倾注了情感和精

力。我曾登过喜马拉雅山和安第斯山，但最引以为傲的还是那堆积成山的手稿，它们字里行间都体现出了我的性格。

两年前，我参与了索尼新一代游戏机平台 PlayStation 2 的泛欧发售。我运用统计软件对消费群体作了划分，利用埃森哲公司的技术解决方案设计了各种形式的市场活动。另外，我还协助开发了一套零售策略，确保能最大限度地获取消费者数据。

作为策略分析师，我们难得看到一个项目从概念进入执行的整个过程。但在这个项目上，我有幸从它发售前数月开始为之工作，直到最后见证了该产品获得巨大的成功。这是欧洲市场上有史以来规模最大的电子产品发售，仅仅在英国，每 5 户家庭中就有一个家庭拥有一台 PlayStation。

这是我在埃森哲公司做了两年的咨询顾问后，第一次负责实质性的任务——领导一条工作流水线。把我的工作成果提交给索尼高层管理人员后，客户对我的工作非常满意，公司也给我升职嘉奖。而且，这个行业作为科技与艺术及商业的结合体让我着迷，我第一次体会到了创意和事业的融合——媒体与娱乐，我找到了属于我的行业。

今年，我抱着慈善的目的去了波斯尼亚一家孤儿院。受到《烽火惊爆线》的感染，我决定去那里看看那些被遗弃的孩子。我看到了一家摇摇欲坠的收容所，里面挤满了孩子，有些孩子身心受过重创。战争期间，这幢楼曾遭受炮击，有些孩子亲眼目睹自己的父母永远地离开了他们，而这家慈善机构的工作人员的爱心和奉献精神深深地打动了我。他们尽其所能地处理着各种事物，靠着梦想和毅力坚持着。我与他们谈话、拍照，答应要帮助他们。

回来之后，我和那家慈善机构共同起草一份意见书送交埃森哲公司，小心地遣词造句，以确保这份意见书能在公司内部产生最大可能的影响。我还在主管人员中进行游说。最后，我们从公司筹到了 4 万美元。后来，这家慈善机构还邀请我去了卢旺达及塞拉利昂。

我为这项成就感到无比自豪。这趟旅行在我父亲过世之前成行。我的父亲生前是英国外交大使，他的一生都致力于为世界各地的外来人员带来安全。他并不太理解我在咨询公司的工作，但那趟旅行之后，我知道他为我感到骄傲。他看到我利用手头的资源对现实作出了改变和贡献。

这次经历，使我决心要为这家慈善机构和埃森哲搭建长久的合作关系，以培养企业社会责任的文化意识。

43
青年创业家

CEO of Company S: Selling a vision to others

One of my biggest accomplishments occurred in 1999, when I turned my vision into a reality, creating a company called Company S. I bootstrapped the company with an initial $14,000 from our first client and over the course of two years, grew the company to a team of eighteen employees. Eventually we raised a first round of financing, expanded our presence into six U.S. cities, and opened our first international office in India, which alone generated $240,000 in new sales over a two-week period. We also created a client list of over one hundred and fifty companies, received free marketing press from more than twenty publications, and faced the opportunity of modifying our business model in a changing economy.

This is an accomplishment in my eyes because I was able to communicate a vision to others, creating a client list of over one hundred and fifty clients despite the fact that we were an inexperienced start-up with a zero-dollar marketing budget. Since we could not afford to advertise, I quickly realized that the best marketing was free press. Articles published in the *Harbus*, *CNET*, and *Boston* magazine gave us the much-needed credibility as we went to sell our services. I was able to sign up companies such as Scient, McKinsey, and Epinions, creating an environment where my employees were inspired and sacrificed higher salaries and worked late hours to help the company reach our goals. Through this experience I realized that by thinking creatively and providing others with a vision, I could be successful.

The Family: Teamwork through rough times

When my father lost his job as a chemical engineer in the 1980s recession, my parents purchased a Laundromat to help pay the bills. During this period, it was essential that our family act as a team both at home and at work. At home, my brother and I split the household chores of laundry, gardening, and cleaning. At work, my brother and father maintained washers and dryers, while my mother and I handed out change, loaded vending machines, and purchased supplies. Every Sunday after finishing my homework, I would spend hours rolling quarters. This experience strengthened our family as a unit. I view this as an accomplishment because I learned the importance of communication and teamwork during tough times. I also gained critical time management skills since I had to balance schoolwork, extracurricular activities, chores, friends, and the business. Finally, this experience taught me the business fundamentals and developed my social skills through my interactions with employees and customers. This experience taught me invaluable skills and laid the foundation for the person I am today.

Advisor for Micro-Enterprise Organization: Giving back to community

In late 2000, I became an advisor for a Bay Area micro-enterprise organization aimed at providing business and technical training to low-income Asian-American women who are starting small businesses. This is a substantial accomplishment for three reasons. First, as a result of my helping the organization define its mission and business plan, it was named a winner in the Craigslist Nonprofit Competition (similar to the private sector Spring Board Venture Capital Award). Second, I am able to serve as an entrepreneurial mentor to women pursuing their visions. Although I was fortunate to have my mother as a mentor, I wished there had been more women role models when starting my own company. In addition, due to my role, the executive director of another organization, an international nonprofit utilizing the digital economy to empower the poor, contacted me to head up their Boston chapter in 2002. By collaborating with these organizations as an advisor, I am influencing both the executive directors and the communities they serve.

Note: Certain identifying information has been changed to preserve confidentiality.

点评

申请人的第一个故事就令人印象深刻：讲述了他如何赤手空拳地创立公司。申请人罗列了一堆事实和数据，它们描绘出一位令人难忘的年轻创业家的生动形象。关键是，文章没有就此停止。申请人继续说道，重点不是他做了什么，而是如何做的。他在本篇Essay中写到，他发现最好的营销方法是免费新闻，展示了他解决实际问题的能力。员工愿意放弃高薪工作而为公司牺牲个人时间的事例，充分展示出了他的激励能力。

申请人选择把成长中的一段经历放在第二位，虽然在时间上向后退了，但是文章在向前发展，因为第二个故事揭示了他为什么是现在的他。第三个成就是关于他为社会作出的贡献的，这表明他具备社会意识，更加完善了申请人年轻领导者的形象。

【参考译文】

S公司的CEO：向他人兜售愿景

我的一个伟大成就是：我在1999年成立了S公司，梦想成真。我用第一位客户付的第一笔收入——14 000美元，开创了这家公司。经过两年的工夫，S公司发展成一家拥有18位员工的企业。我们终于募到了第一笔融资，于是在美国的6大城市分别设立了分公司，又在印度开设了第一家境外办事处。光是印度办事处，就在两周创下了24万美元的销售额。我们还整理了一份列有150多家公司的客户名单，收到了20多家出版社寄来的免费市场报道。在日益变化的市场环境中，我们面临着调整商业模式的机遇。

我认为这是我的成就，因为我为同事描绘了一个愿景。尽管我们是一家刚起步又没经验的公司，而且没有一分钱的市场营销预算，但是我们拥有150多家客户名单。由于付不起广告费，我立马想到最好的营销渠道是免费的报纸杂志。在推销我们的服务时，发表在*Harbus*、*CNET*和《波士顿》杂志上的文章给了我们急需的公信力。我能够和诸如施恩、麦肯锡还有Epinions这样的公司签约，营造出激励人心的工作环境。员工自愿放弃其他高薪工作，为公司共同的目标加班加点。从这段经验中，我认识到成功在于创造性的思维以及为他人描绘一个愿景。

家庭：团结互助，共渡难关

20世纪80年代经济大萧条时，我的父亲丢掉了化学工程师的工作。父母买下一家洗衣店以贴补家用。这段时期，重要的是全家人在工作、生活中齐心协力。在家里，我也由此和哥哥平分洗衣服、修剪花木和打扫房间这些家务活。工作中，哥哥和父亲要操作洗衣机和烘干机，而母亲和我负责找零、给自动售货机填货、采购补给等。每个星期天做完功课后，我要花几个小时的时间卷硬币。这段经历使我们家越发团结，我也由此懂得了沟通和团队合作在困难时期的重要性，因此，我把它看作一个成就。由于我必须平衡在学业、课外活动、家务、朋友以及家里小生意上投入的时间，我还学会了重要的时间管理技能。最后，这段经历让我明白了基本的商业原则，并在与员工、客户打交道的过程中锻炼了我的社交技能，从中学到的宝贵技能为成就今天的我奠定了基础。

小型企业组织的顾问：回馈社会

2000年年底，我成了海湾地区一家小型企业组织的一名顾问，该组织的宗旨，是为打算做小生意的低收入亚裔美籍妇女提供业务和技术培训。这是一项重大成就，原因有三：第一，我帮该组织界定了自己的使命，制订了业务计划。结果，该组织赢得了克雷格列表网站的非营利性组织比赛（类似于春季理事会创投奖的私营板块）。第二，作为创业导师，我负责为那些追求理想的妇女提供指导。虽然我本人很幸运有母亲作我的导师，但在我创业之初，也曾希望有更多的女性榜样可以学习。第三，鉴于我的能力，另一家非营利性组织的执行总裁邀请我在2002年领导他们在波士顿的业务，这家组织的主要工作是利用数字经济提高贫困人群的自主权。我作为顾问和两家机构通力合作，既对双方的执行总裁产生了影响，又对他们服务的人群产生了影响。①

① 为了保密，已经更改了申请人的某些身份信息。

44
在寻根之旅中追寻个人意义

Finding my Irish Heritage

I've never felt more fulfilled than when I visited my family's ancestral home in Ireland for the first time. In my diverse international experiences, I had never directly encountered my own family's rich cultural heritage. So, after years of playing the Irish fiddle and listening to my granny's stories of Uncle Johnny the fiddler, I traveled to the very farm where my granny grew up. I played soccer with cousins I had only seen in pictures, visited my great-grandfather's grave, and saw the school-house where my granny completed her second-grade education.

After showing me around the farm, my cousins insisted on finding me a fiddle to play. The local musician happened to have just restored Uncle Johnny's fiddle. We borrowed it and I played "Shoe the Donkey" and other favorites on my great-great-granduncle's fiddle. The emotion of playing this fiddle was tremendous—it embodied a physical and emotional connection between past and present—yet it fell far short of the joy I felt in recounting the story to my granny. As a result of my family pilgrimage, my granny left this world two years later knowing that Uncle Johnny's legacy was alive and well.

McKinsey: From Consulting to Operations

During my second year at McKinsey, I led a four-person client team through a successful home heating oil-marketing pilot that convinced me that I could be a manager and not just a consultant.

The week before the pilot, the client team leader Gerry got called out of town. Having led the pilot design, I was the natural selection to manage the first week of the rollout from Gerry's office. Dedication and integrity earlier in the project gave me the organizational credibility to assume the role of manager, which was essential for the successful execution of the tasks at hand. I worked with Gerry's five-person staff to organize and analyze the early pilot results, fielded questions from twenty-six branch managers, sent out daily updates, and coached managers who were falling behind. As operational glitches emerged, I mobilized the necessary corporate departments to develop quick solutions. During that first week of the pilot, I helped a two-hundred-and-fifty-person organization realize its potential to implement a project rapidly and effectively. At the same time, I discovered my own ability to manage and execute at the helm of a large operation.

Personal Impact in Portugal

In 1997, I won a Fulbright Scholarship to study African immigration to Portugal. Despite the relaxed requirements of the program, I defined my own rigorous framework for the year. I identified a gap in the current literature on immigrant transnationalism and focused my research on Guinea-Bissauan immigrants' efforts to support development projects in their home villages. My work was subsequently published in the journal of *South European Society & Politics*.

Publishing my research was a tangible measure of my achievements in Portugal, yet for me success was demonstrated by the personal impact that I had on the very immigrants I was researching. I created and led volunteer English classes for African college students and started a community youth center's first-ever physical education program. As a measure of the trust I developed with the community, I was asked to serve as a *portador*, or courier of money and material goods from immigrants to their families, during my field research trip to Guinea-Bissau. In doing so, I was able to connect immigrants with their families only three months before they lost all contact due to the outbreak of civil war in Guinea-Bissau. These unique personal contributions transformed intellectual endeavor into action and no doubt informed my larger transition from consultant to nonprofit manager two years later.

点 评

申请人领着读者经历了他人生中的三件大事，每件事都是一次自我发现。通过一次个人的追寻、一项商业试验以及一次义工经历，申请人向读者提供了三个视角来了解他视为重要的东西。

在第一个故事中，申请人将他多姿多彩的环球阅历与他早就该成行的爱尔兰小镇寻根之旅对照，然后又描述了这趟旅行对他祖母的影响。在第二个故事中，申请人说，尽管别人看到的可能是这个试验项目的成功，而他收获的则是挖掘了自己的领导才干。在第三个故事中，申请人描述了他如何为获得富布赖特奖学金而自豪。自豪原因并非是因为他的作品得到了发表，而是因为他改变了移民的生活。三个故事都非常优秀，不仅故事本身令人印象深刻，而且申请人向读者解释了这些成就为什么对他个人很重要。从中学到的教训是，不要以为缺乏个人意义描写的成就可以同样吸引人。尽管你的成就可能令人高山仰止，但真正的价值却是让录取委员会了解什么对你来说才是重要的。

【参考译文】

寻找我的爱尔兰根

第一次，我回到了我的祖先在爱尔兰的家，这一经历让我从来不曾如此满足过。在我丰富多彩的环球阅历中，我从来没有直接面对过自己家族那深厚的文化遗产。因此，在我拉了数年的爱尔兰小提琴，以及听奶奶讲了很多遍有关小提琴家约翰尼叔叔的故事后，我来到了奶奶长大的那个农场。我和我那位只在照片中见过的堂兄一起踢足球，去曾祖父的墓前祭奠了一番，并参观了奶奶读了两年书的学校。

堂兄带我在农场转悠了一圈之后，坚持要给我找一把小提琴拉一拉。当地的音乐家正好修好了约翰尼叔叔的小提琴，我们就借了这把小提琴——曾曾叔父的小提琴，拉了一曲 *Shoe the Donkey* 以及其他几首我喜欢的曲子。演奏这把小提琴时，我的内心汹涌澎湃，因为它是在物质上和情感上联接过去和现在的象征，不过这仍远比不上我向奶奶讲述这个故事时感受到的喜悦。奶奶得知约翰尼叔叔的遗物仍然保存完好，因此在这趟家族本源寻根之旅的两年后安然离世了。

麦肯锡，从咨询走向运作

在麦肯锡工作的第二年，我带领一支4人的客户团队，成功地完成了一个家用燃油营销的试点项目。这次经历让我相信自己可以成为一名经理，而不仅仅是一名咨询师。

项目开始前一周，客户团队领导格里被安排出差。由于这个试点项目是我负责设计的，我自然而然地进驻格里的办公室，负责第一周的首期展示。在项目早期，我所展现的投入和正直品质让组织内部相信我能胜任经理这个角色，这种信任是成功执行手头任务的基础。我与格里的5人小组齐心协力，组织并分析初期试验的结果，回答26位分部经理的问题，每天寄出更新的材料并指导掉队的经理。当出现操作故障时，我调动相关的公司部门迅速解决了问题。在项目启动的第一周里，我帮助这家250人的公司认识到自己有潜力快速、有效地执行项目。同时，我也发现了自己在大型项目领导岗位上的管理和执行能力。

对葡萄牙移民的影响

1997年，我赢得了富布赖特奖学金，用以研究葡萄牙的非洲移民。尽管研究项目的要求很松，但是我为这一年制订了严格的计划。我发现，在现今的文学世界中，空缺了移民的跨国主义这个主题，于是，我把自己的研究重点放在几内亚比绍移民如何支持家乡发展的成就上。我的研究成果随后发表在《南欧社会和政治》杂志上。

研究成果得以发表，是衡量我在葡萄牙的成就的一个切实标准，然而对我来说，成功更在于我影响了我所研究的移民群体。我创立并领导了面向非洲大学生的义务英语班，并在一家社区青少年中心发起了第一个体育项目。作为我赢得了社区信任的佐证，在我前往几内亚比绍作现场调查时，我受邀成为一名"portador"，即替移民往家乡捎带金钱和物品的使者。通过我，这些移民能够和他们的家人联系上。就在三个月前，几内亚比绍爆发内战，他们与家人之间的联系断绝了。这些独特的个人贡献将智力上的努力转变为行动，同时，毫无疑问地，也预示了我两年后的更大的转变——从咨询顾问到非营利性组织的经理。

45
主动性才是真正的成就

The Yale Daily News (YDN)

As publisher and president of the *Yale Daily News*, I led the organization to record profits. I introduced a new source of revenue by negotiating a landmark contract with Simon & Schuster to publish five reference books for high school and college students. I also revamped the circulation of the paper, creating a more cost-effective system. Lastly, I recruited a larger sales force, leading to stronger advertising sales. The increased profits enabled us to introduce color printing and an expanded daily paper and to contribute to the *YDN's* endowment for the first time in a decade.

I consider my tenure as publisher and president of the *Yale Daily News* a substantial accomplishment for several reasons. Without any formal business education, I led the organization to new heights while balancing other leadership positions. While publisher, I worked forty hours per week at the *YDN*. Despite this significant time commitment, I successfully served as president of my sorority and senior society and organized a tutoring program. In order to manage the *YDN* and my other responsibilities, I learned how to prioritize tasks, delegate projects, and manage others.

I cherish my experience as publisher of the *YDN* because it demonstrated to me my ability to lead effectively and shaped my professional aspirations to run an organization.

Competitive Intelligence

When I began working in Morgan Stanley's retail brokerage division, I was shocked by the dearth of competitor and industry knowledge. We could not improve our business model without better understanding industry trends and our position relative to the competition.

After identifying this gap, I conceived *Competitive Intelligence*, a biweekly newsletter designed to detail competitor news and industry trends. I created a template, determined my audience, selected appropriate categories of news, and identified relevant news sources. I presented my business case and a sample issue to the division's president. He immediately approved the program. From the initial issue, the feedback was overwhelmingly positive. The distribution of *Competitive Intelligence* has grown from fifteen to one thousand employees since the newsletter's introduction, demonstrating its relevance and success.

I am proud of my efforts to establish *Competitive Intelligence* because I successfully identified a need within the division, developed an appropriate tool to fill the need, and have consistently executed a quality product. As a result of *Competitive Intelligence*, senior management is more knowledgeable about our competitive position, and I am often consulted as the resident expert on the competition. However, I take the greatest pride in the initiative I took to create *Competitive Intelligence* and consider that the true accomplishment.

Student/Sponsor Partners (S/SP)

In September 2000, through S/SP, I began sponsoring Kimberly, a high school freshman from the Bronx. While I immediately liked Kim, we struggled to connect. Nonetheless, I faithfully called Kim every two weeks to monitor her adjustment to high school. I closely followed her academic progress and provided her with supplementary study materials. During the school year, we met every six weeks. Hoping that Kim would share more about herself, I exposed Kim to some of my interests, such as visiting art exhibits and museums. Gradually, as I demonstrated my commitment and friendship to her, Kim opened up. Today, we have established a true bond and are important parts of one another's lives. I am proud to serve as a positive role model for Kim. Although the academic and financial support I provide is critical to Kim's academic success, I consider my dedication and loyalty to Kim the most noteworthy accomplishment.

These three accomplishments highlight four qualities I value highly: leadership, initiative, dedication, and loyalty.

点评

本文组织得当，条理清晰。申请人系统地介绍了他的三大成就，先介绍情况，然后中肯地评价这些成就的重要性。因此，文章详尽地展现了该话题的核心要点。

但是，文章极端结构化也有其危险之处。申请人选择的事例符合标准的成就三重唱——课外活动、职业以及社区服务，可以在许多文章中见到。重复使用同一套结构（成就加解释），可能使这些成就黯淡无光。所幸的是，本文的每个事例都非常有料，掩盖了结构老套这一弱点。内容再一次胜过形式。

【参考译文】

《耶鲁每日新闻》

作为《耶鲁每日新闻》出品人和发行人，我带领该报社创下了营业利润最高额的纪录。我开拓了一项新收入来源：首次与西蒙与舒斯特出版社签约出版5本大学生和高中生使用的参考书。我还改革了报纸的发行系统，建立了一套更节约成本并有效益的体系。最后，我还扩充了报社的销售队伍，广告销售节节攀升。利润提高后，我们可以引进彩色印刷，增加日报版面，而且也为《耶鲁每日新闻》十年来第一次捐赠作出了贡献。

我把自己在《耶鲁每日新闻》担任出品人和发行人视为一项重大成就，有如下几条原因。虽然我没接受过任何正规的商业教育，却能够带领该社达到新的高度，同时我还要兼顾其他领导职务。我在《耶鲁每日新闻》报社每周工作40小时。尽管投入了大量的时间，我仍然出色地完成了高年级学生联谊会主席的工作，并组织了一个学习帮带项目。为了完成《耶鲁每日新闻》及其他工作，我学会了如何分配任务的优先级，如何授权给其他人，以及如何管理下属等。

我非常珍惜作为《耶鲁每日新闻》发行人的这段经历，因为它证明了我具备领导才能并坚定了我的职业抱负——创业。

《竞争对手追踪》

加入摩根士丹利的零售经纪部门后，我惊讶地发现，本部门对竞争对手的信息和行业知识竟然如此无知。如果不深入了解行业发展趋势，不认识自身在市场竞争中所处的位置，我们就不可能改善商业模式。

发现这个不足后，我着手编辑了一份半月刊《竞争对手追踪》，收集有关竞争对手的新闻和行业发展趋势。我设计了模板，设定了目标读者群，挑选了几类适合的新闻，并确定了相关的新闻来源。然后将一份样刊连同我的名片呈送部门主任审阅，他马上批准了此项目。从第一期半月刊发出起，好评如潮。自《竞争对手追踪》问世以来，这份半月刊的订阅人数从15人发展到1 000人，足以证明其实用性与成功。

准确捕捉部门内部的需求，开发合适的工具以满足需求，并持续送出高质量的刊物——我为自己投入在《竞争对手追踪》上的心血而自豪。有了《竞争对手追踪》，高层管理者对公司的竞争优势更加明晰，而我也经常被邀请作为内部的竞争市场专家出谋划策。但最令我引以为傲的是我在创办《竞争对手追踪》上体现的主动性，这才是真正的成就。

学生－资助人项目（S/SP项目）

2000年9月，我开始通过S/SP项目资助金伯莉的学业。她是一名出生在布朗克斯的高一学生。虽然我立刻喜欢上了小金，但她却不能向我敞开心扉。即便如此，我仍然雷打不动地每两周给小金打一次电话，了解她是否适应高中生活。我还密切关注她的学习进度，常给她送去学习辅导材料。那一学年里，我们每6周聚会一次。为了让小金多聊聊自己，我告诉她自己的兴趣爱好，比如参观艺术展、博物馆等。精诚所至，金石为开，她渐渐地敞开了心扉。今天，我们之间已经建立了真正的纽带，视彼此为对方生命中的重要组成部分。我为

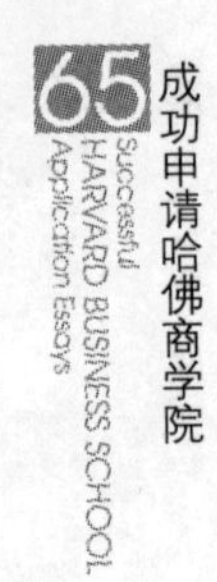

自己能够成为小金的积极榜样而骄傲。虽然我对小金的学业和金钱的支持是她取得优良成绩的关键因素，但是我认为，自己对她的奉献和忠诚才是最值得关注的成就。

上述这三大成就凸显了我非常重视的4项素质：领导力、主动性、奉献和忠诚。

46
移民日本的“老外”

The Japanese language is highly complex. Two alphabets and a large number of kanji (characters) must be memorized, and respect for one's elders reflected in the grammar itself: to mistake this is to risk insult. At age seventeen, after five years of study at high school in Australia, I came to Japan with a few rudimentary phrases and four hundred kanji—the average Japanese high school student knows more than two thousand.

My move to Japan in April 1993 represented a great academic challenge—to attend lectures, research, and study under the same conditions as a native at a Japanese university—but also a personal opportunity, a tremendous chance to broaden my horizons. Five years in a foreign country and culture by myself was a daunting prospect, but I took the view that if I could not cope, I could always return to Australia fluent in Japanese after the one-year intensive language training course. The experience was both more challenging and rewarding than I had imagined.

The first year at Kyoto University was particularly tough academically. Although Japanese language school prepared me for the grammar and vocabulary needed, I was overwhelmed at first by the sheer amount of work required, taking two hours, for example, to read what took my Japanese classmates half an hour. Not only was I studying new concepts, but in a foreign language; a novel experience was to learn German and Chinese from a Japanese base. It was slow and painstaking work. However, I refused to give up, setting myself arbitrary high standards. I used English books to study together with the Japanese texts, borrowed friends' notes to fill in the gaps I had missed in lectures, and with perseverance my language ability and grades improved.

At university, a classmate asked me to join a newly established amateur musical drama group. I had performed in musicals and youth operas in Australia and was keen to join. We did everything ourselves, from creating the dialogue (in Japanese), music and dance routines, to backstage work (making costumes, sets, and lighting), to ticketing and marketing. The first performance had an audience of only one hundred in a crude yet intimate setting, but with time out productions increased in scale and hugely improved in quality. My strength is singing, and I am particularly proud that the vocal training regimens I implemented helped the group cope with the acoustics of the increasingly larger venues. I was also rapt when after one production I received a message addressed to the "foreign-looking detective" complimenting my performance. By my senior year, the group's performance was an established part of the Kyoto University Students' Festival, in a hall seating over one thousand people.

Upon graduation, I decided to work for a Japanese trading company. Many foreign students return home at that stage claiming some expertise in Japanese culture, but I realized I lacked the needed experience in Japanese business culture. I entered the company—only the second Westerner to do so—with much thc same attitude that I had five years earlier: I have nothing to lose.

From the beginning I was treated no differently, expected to pet-form to the level of my peers. I appreciated and accepted the challenge, and I believe rose to it. Not only have I come to understand Japanese customs—reporting techniques and the etiquette required in business discussions, for example—but also the Japanese way of thinking. However, this has not been to the detriment to my Western side. I believe I have maintained a global perspective and balance between cultures necessary for international business.

点评

申请人没有罗列三个独立的成就故事，而是记叙了他如何决定来日本学习并最终在日本工作的。尽管移居国外这件事本身没什么特别（许多申请人都做过），但申请人解释了为什么在日本学习和生活具有挑战性，从而为本文设定了舞台。从这三个故事中，我们看到了一个意志坚定、持之以恒的申请人，为了充分利用逆境，愿意全力以赴。虽然他承认，如果在日本待不下去了，他很容易就可以回国，但是我们发现，申请人绝不是一个轻言放弃的人，除非他达成了设定的目标。

第三个成就故事可能是最不吸引人的，尽管这个故事强调了申请人以开放的心态和坚定的意志对待新环境，但它没有讲太多他对公司的贡献。如果申请人能把笔墨更多地放在他对公司的贡献上，而不是以一句模棱两可的句子（“这些无损我作为西方人的一面”）作为结尾，那么本篇 Essay 会更有说服力。

不过，总的来说，这是一篇优秀的范文，它将三项成就编织成一个紧密连贯的故事，对比那些结构传统的 Essay，即描述一系列大体上独立的成就故事，这样的结构效果很好。

【参考译文】

日语是一门极其复杂的语言。学习这门语言必须牢记平假名和片假名两组字母，还需要掌握海量的日本汉字；对长辈的尊敬还体现在语法里面——在这上面出错会有侮辱他人的危险。17 岁那年，在澳大利亚读完了五年的高中，我来到了日本。我的语言储备是一点点初级短语和 400 个日本汉字——普通日本高中生认识 2 000 多个日本汉字。

我在 1993 年 4 月搬去日本，这既是一个极大的学术挑战——在一家日本大学跟日本人一样上课、调研、学习，也是我个人的一个机会，一个扩展我视野的好机会。孤身一人在异国他乡生活 5 年，想想就让人心生畏惧，但我紧紧抓住这个想法：纵使我万一熬不下去，我还能回到澳大利亚，且经过一年的强化语言训练，至少练就了一口流利的日语。那段经历不仅比我想象得更具挑战性，收获也更丰厚。

第一年在京都大学的学习尤其艰辛。虽然日本语言学校为我准备了所需的语法和词汇，但是一开始，单单是作业量就把我压得喘不过气了。比如，日本同学半个小时的阅读量，我得花两个小时。我不仅要学习新的概念，而且还要用外语学习，用日语学习德文和中文就是一种新体验。这项工作漫长且痛苦，可我拒绝放弃，执意给自己制订高标准。我用英文教科书和日文教学书对照着学习，借朋友的笔记补自己上课时漏掉的内容，终于，我的坚持换来了语言能力和分数的提高。

读大学时，一位同学邀请我加入新近成立的业余音乐剧社团。我在澳洲的时候曾演过音乐剧和青少年歌剧，所以十分渴望加入。我们一手操办了全部事情：从编对话（用日语）、谱曲、排舞，到后台的工作（缝制戏服、舞台布景，以及灯光），再到售票和推广。第一场演出只来了100位观众，场景虽简陋但气氛温馨。而随着时间的推移，我们的作品不仅在规模上增加了，质量也得到了长足的提高。我的长项是歌唱，而令我尤其自豪的是，我负责的声乐强化训练帮助队员们解决了随着场地变大而产生的声学问题。一场演出之后，我收到了一张注明写给“老外侦探”的卡片，称赞我的精彩表演。等到我大四那年，这个社团的演出成了京都大学学生节的固定节目，而且是在一个坐了1 000多名观众的大厅里演出。

毕业后，我决定在一家日本贸易公司工作。很多外国留学生这时都回国了，声称自己是日本某文化方面的专家，但我意识到，我还缺乏所需的日本商业文化方面的经验。我进入这家公司（该公司的第二个外国人）的想法跟我5年前的想法差不多：我没什么好失去的。

从一开始，公司就对我一视同仁，期望我发挥与同事一样的工作水平。我接受了这个挑战，并且心怀感激，我相信我能胜任这个挑战。我不仅理解了日本的商业风俗（比如向上级汇报的技巧及商务会谈中所需的礼节），还掌握了日本商人的思维方式，然而，这些无损我作为西方人的一面。我相信，我已经培养了一种全球化的观点，并找到了在国际贸易中所需的文化平衡。

STRENGTHS AND WEAKNESSES

命题7
优点与缺点

Provide a candid assessment of your strengths and weaknesses.

请对你的强项和弱项作出中肯的评价。

解题思路

如同构思其他命题一样，描述优缺点之前的第一步是明确评价你是谁。虽然你很难同时成为“最崇拜自己的人”和“最苛刻的批评家”，但是此话题给了你一个机会以证明你了解你自己。坦诚很重要，不要假装谦逊，也不要胡乱吹嘘。没必要害羞，但是要实话实说。

罗列优点没多大难度，但是要你描述缺点，你可能就不知道从何下手了。不过，可以把它当成一个展示个人及职业发展的机会，过去、未来都行。选择一个缺点（不是变相的优点），然后说明你如何意识到这个缺点的存在、它如何影响你的生活，以及你是如何克服它的。如此一来，读者会认为你是一个成熟且有自知之明的人。另一方面，不要选择一些影响你被录取的缺点，比如害怕公众演讲。

后面的文章展示了描述优缺点可能采取的多种方式。使用具体事例作支撑往往效果最好。如果运用得当，列举个性特征的方式也非常有效。写作风格可正式也可随意，可思辨也可诗意，只要你的表达自信、真诚。请注意，一篇优秀的文章，其形式既能表现内容，又能强化内容。

最后请记住，虽然你是在评价自己的个性，但同时也在申请哈佛商学院。如果你能够指出自己的优点可以给学校带去价值，而影响你发展的缺点可以通过哈佛的 MBA 课程加以改进，那么，没人会轻视你的文章。

点评人： 拉莫尼卡·卡彭特（LaMonica Carpenter）

47
人贵有自知之明

Above all, I am passionate. I hunger for knowledge and truth. I follow through with reading and debate until I am satisfied with my level of understanding. I learn quickly. I integrate disparate concepts with relative ease. I avoid jumping to conclusions. Once convinced, I will fight for my point of view. Once proven wrong, I am equally happy to accept the opposing conclusion. When I cannot find the answer, or I know that another would excel where I am weak, I am quick to recognize my limitations and seek assistance. These strengths enable me to problem-solve efficiently and completely.

I write well. I speak well. I am persuasive in my communications with peers, superiors, and clients. I am able to learn languages quickly, and retain the ability while dormant.

I am warm and full of empathy, but lack emotional engagement in business. People like me. I am able to see the best in everyone and still recognize the warning signs of dishonesty, insecurity, and imperfect intentions. I am very loyal to those who earn my loyalty.

Still, I am not patient. I like to move quickly, sometimes more quickly than is prudent. In my haste, I am prone to forget or disregard protocol. In my haste, I might not communicate as completely as I should.

I am a perfectionist. I am overly self-critical and often demand more of myself than is possible. I expect nearly as much of others as of myself. I am outspoken and quick to speak, even when a period of calm or silence would best resolve the situation.

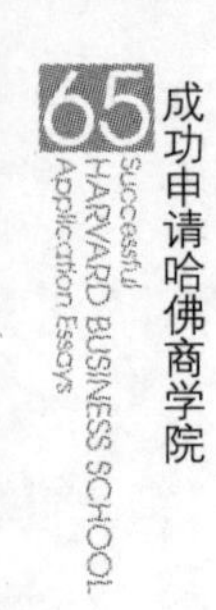

I have difficulty working for someone whom I don't respect, or for a cause in which I don't believe. I will not lie or fib to please others, and instead sometimes air my opinions when silent agreement would expedite the accomplishment of the task at hand.

Finally, I have gaps in my business training and business skills. In investment banking and private equity I have employed financial analysis skills, and yet my understanding is incomplete due to limited financial coursework. I have on-the-job experience, but have not undergone a training program or classical academic business training. I have built up industry understanding in wireless software and a few other areas, but I do not have in-depth knowledge of most areas of business or the broad perspective gained by study of a comprehensive business curriculum.

点 评

本文在传达申请人的个性和品质方面表现杰出。独特的意识流风格使本文出类拔萃。全文没有开场也没有收尾，这种写作方式很有风险，但又彰显了申请人的个性。申请人把个性特征一条条罗列成文，似乎无休无止，但这样的方式让读者生出更多的期待。多数文章可能会集中讲述少数几个优缺点，而本文申请人却铺天盖地撒出一堆小事，覆盖了不同寻常的广度，同时没有给人自高自大的感觉。这种写作风格反映了他的个性——正体现了他雄辩却缺少耐心这一性格特征，说到底，申请人是一个非常有自知之明的人。

介绍缺点的段落与优点一样细致。申请人暗示，克服这些缺点与他的职业生涯息息相关。申请人总结说，他需要接受正规的商业训练，这给人留下了清晰的印象。不用直说，申请人已经向录取委员会表明进入哈佛商学院学习将是个人发展的重要一步。

【参考译文】

首先，我是个热情洋溢的人。我对知识和真理的渴求如饥似渴，通过阅读和辩论追本溯源，直到我透彻理解为止。学习快，能做到融会贯通。我绝不草率下结论：如果确信观点正确，我会奋力捍卫；如果被证明有误，我也乐于接受对方的结论。当我找不到答案时，若明确对方比我更擅长解决某个问题，我能够迅速看到自己的局限性并寻求帮助。以上这些优点有利于我彻底、有效地解决问题。

我的写作能力很好，演讲能力也不错。与同事、上司及客户沟通时，非常有说服力。我擅长学习语言，即使搁置不用，也能维持原有水平。

我对人诚挚亲切，充满同情心，但是对事情缺少情感投入。人人都喜欢我。我能欣赏他人的优秀，也能识破对方的谎言和不良企图，能看出对方可靠与否。对于值得我效忠的人，我非常忠诚。

不过，我缺乏耐心，往往冒进、急躁，有时效率有余，谨慎不足。匆忙中，我常常丢三落四，甚至忽视常规。我的沟通可能有所欠缺。

我是个完美主义者。严于律己，常常挑战极限。我总是以对待自己的标准要求他人。直言不讳，快言快语，尽管有些时候，沉默或安静才是最好的解决方式。

我很难在我不敬重的人手下工作，也不能为一个我不相信的目标奋斗。我不会虚言奉承，即便是无伤大雅的说辞；有时沉默接受可能会加速完成手头的任务，但我还是会提出自己的观点。

最后，我在商务训练和商务技巧方面仍然有待提高。在投资银行和私人股权融资方面，我掌握了财务分析技能，但是由于金融方面的课程作业有限，因此，我对它的认识仍不够全面。我拥有实际工作经验，但是没参加过培训项目，也不曾学过经典的商业知识。我懂得无线软件等方面的行业知识，但是对与商业相关的多数领域了解不深，也缺乏综合商业训练所培养的全局思维。

48
规划未来 VS 风险厌恶

I explored my character and confronted perceptions of myself with reality by asking closest friends about my strengths and weaknesses. They uniformly mentioned maturity, ambition, and logical thinking as my greatest assets. These characteristics have been reflected in my strategic approach to life. Since high school, I have thought five or ten years forward, set challenging goals and persistently achieved them. For instance, I managed a Boy Scout unit not just because it was fun and gave me satisfaction, but also because it gave me leadership practice early in my career. I learned foreign languages in anticipation of international assignments and eventual opening of the Polish marketplace. I also established an investment fund to gain hands-on experience in investing. Privately, I particularly pride myself in the ability to connect and work effectively with people from various backgrounds and cultures, be it top managers, politicians or artists. I successfully coached inner-city youth at a summer camp in Poland. I have worked in offices in Europe, Asia, and the U.S., and I was equally professional in each environment due to my flexibility and eagerness to learn about new cultures. I have always taken care to maintain and develop personal relationships. Despite recent extensive business travels, I have stayed in touch with my friends and colleagues.

On the other hand, I wish I were more willing to take risks. This feature may be a derivative of my recent position as acting project risk manager, where I was responsible for recognizing and evaluating all potential risk areas in project-financed transactions. I recognize that risk aversion was advantageous in my risk management job. However, at this early stage in my career and life, I believe I should be more of a risk-taker to benefit from my still steep learning curve, while experiencing new processes and practices. Therefore, I intend to continually take new challenges in business, which is reflected in my plans to eventually establish business incubators and/or a foundation in Poland. In stressful situations, I tend to be overly critical and demanding of myself and others. My exactness may be fastidious to subordinates and colleagues, so I strive to "loosen up" and be more patient without sacrificing the quality of work. I am working on being able to identify the optimal level of meticulousness in each task, and to motivate others to do their best under tense circumstances.

点评

诚实、可信是本篇Essay无可争议的优点。在第一段，申请人与读者分享了自己花费很多精力来进行自我挖掘，这使得他与众不同。他不仅通过自省的方式来认识自己的优点和缺点，还请他最亲近的朋友来帮忙，这表明他不仅很有自知之明，还乐于接受他人的建设性意见。他的优点深深扎根于从小培养的性格中，并且用了一系列详细的例子来阐释这些优点如何影响他生活的方方面面。

申请人成功地描绘了大量有关他生活经历及个性人格的细节，并使之互为补充。在本篇精心撰写的Essay中，每一个词、每一个例子都给他的优缺点增加了可信度。读者在读完第一段后就对申请人的个性有了深刻的认识，所以我们很轻松就明白了他的缺点为什么是真实的缺点，而非伪装的优点。比如，他不愿承担风险与他细心规划未来的优点是相通的，他用一则轶事来支撑这个缺点，并详细说明了他克服该缺点的方法。对于如此坦白的一份自我评估，我们很难加以质疑。

【参考译文】

我请最亲近的朋友描述我的优缺点，以此来挖掘我的性格，用事实挑战我的自我认知。他们无一例外地提到，成熟、事业心和逻辑思维是我最宝贵的缺点。这些性格特征体现在我对待生活的战略性方法上。从高中起，我已经规划了未来5年或10年之后的事情，设定具有挑战性的目标，并坚持完成这些目标。比如，我带领过一个童子军团，不仅因为它有趣，给我满足感，也因为它给处于事业初期的我提供了锻炼领导力的机会。我学习外语，期望国际合作，并最终打开波兰市场。我还设立了投资基金，以获得投资方面的实战经验。私底下，我为自己的人际交往能力感到自豪，我能有效地与来自不同文化背景的人熟识并一起工作，无论是高级经理、政客，还是艺术家。我在波兰一个内陆城市的青少年夏令营做教练，而且相当成功。我曾在欧洲、亚洲以及美国的办公室上过班。由于我的灵活性和了解新文化的热情，我不管在哪里都同样敬业。我总是小心地开发和维护个人关系。尽管最近频繁出差，我依然与朋友、同事保持联系。

另一方面，我希望自己能更主动地承担风险。这个性格特征可能是我最近成为项目的代理风险管理经理后产生的。在那个项目中，我负责识别并评估项目融资交易中所有潜在的风险领域。我发现，厌恶风险对于风险管理工作是个优势，然而，在我人生及职场生涯的早期，我认为自己更应该做一个敢于冒险的人，以体验新的过程和实践，在学习中获得收益。因此，我想要在生意场上不断接受新的挑战，这也体现在我希望最终在波兰建立商业孵化器以及基金会的计划中。在高压下，我常会对自己和他人过于苛求。我的严格可能对下属和同事来讲过于挑剔，因而，我尽力在不降低工作质量的前提下“放松”，并且更加耐心。我正努力学习了解每项任务最合适的严厉程度，并激励他人在压力下尽力而为。

49
优势即劣势

I think that enthusiastic, professional, and international, with all the positive and negative implications, would be a good way to summarize my strengths and weaknesses. When I decide to take something on, whether in business or in personal life, I tend to be very enthusiastic about it: I want to give it my best, get as much as possible out of it, and enjoy myself while doing so. I put my heart into everything I do. Therefore, enthusiasm is one of my biggest strengths: it makes it easy for me to get on with anyone, to motivate people, and to create a fun and supportive environment around me. My positive nature has also helped me to get through tough times (whether on projects or during difficult company situations). However, enthusiasm is also one of my weaknesses by making me relatively impatient with people that have a negative or cynical outlook. Because I fully engage in anything I do, a cynical attitude goes against what I stand for and believe in. Therefore, I find it more emotionally challenging to deal with people who have a more neutral attitude towards their work.

I would also describe myself as professional. When I take on a task, I want to do it to the best of my ability and make no compromises. I find it crucially important to be respectful among colleagues and towards superiors and clients, especially in today's sometimes very casual workplace. Professionalism makes me a thorough and appreciated colleague, who provides robust and well-considered analyses and conclusions. However, this very thoroughness and perfectionism sometimes prevents me from taking on tasks that I feel I have too little experience in. Although I am always ready to take on challenges when I have the fight support mechanism, I never make bullish statements about my abilities unless I am convinced I am well prepared to do the job, sometimes leading me to underestimate my abilities.

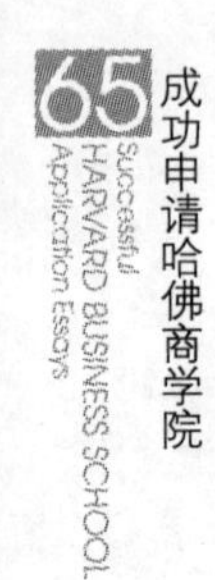

Finally, being international is also both a strength and a weakness. Having traveled a lot during my studies and my work has given me a lot of confidence of being able to stand on my own, even in a foreign environment. I cherish international contact. On the downside, being very international has left me less deeply rooted in any one place than people who have spent their entire lives in the same community.

点 评

申请人指出，他的三大优势即是他的三大弱势，这种方式别具一格，反响不俗。优势发展到极致会变成弱势，如此简单说来可能会让人感觉申请人含糊其辞，但申请人在文中给出具体事例作详细解释，使文章赢得了认同。申请人提供了三例具体的私人经历来说明他的观点，因此，文章除了描述他的优缺点，还表明申请人是一位有自知之明的，成熟的，生活、工作两不误的人。

用非标准的写作方式完成申请命题总是有风险的。构思时过于无视格式会使人感觉文章偏离中心话题。然而，如果运用得当，则可以使你的文章脱颖而出。

【参考译文】

我认为，热情、职业化、国际化这三个词语所包含的正反两方面的含义，恰好可以总结我的优点和缺点。当我下定决心做某事的时候，无论是工作上的还是个人生活方面的，往往都干劲十足：我愿意全力以赴做到最好，同时享受过程带给我的乐趣。我用心去做每件事，因此，热情是我最大的优势之一：热情的个性让我很容易与他人相处，我总是激励身边的人，并在我的周围营造出一个轻松、互助的环境。积极的天性也帮我度过了不少艰难时光（无论是在项目进行的过程中，还是当公司陷入困境时）。然而，热情也是我的弱点之一，它让我对消极或者愤世嫉俗的人缺乏耐心。因为我总是全身心地投入到我所做的事情中去，因而冷嘲热讽的态度不符合我的立场和信仰，所以对我来说，与那些对工作无所谓的人相处，在情感上是更大的挑战。

我也自认为是一个有职业素养的人。工作时我全力以赴，决不将就。我认为，尊重同事、上司和客户十分重要，尤其是在当今一些非常随意的工作环境中。职业精神使我办事仔细，懂得欣赏同事，可以提出缜密的分析和结论。不过有时，正是这种彻底的完美主义妨碍我尝试经验不足的新任务。当我拥有完备的承受机制时，我总是随时备战。但我从不自我吹嘘，除非我坚信自己已经为此做足了准备，但有时这也会导致我低估自己的能力。

最后，国际化也是好坏参半。我在读书、工作时曾去过很多地方，对自己独立生活的能力充满信心，甚至在一个陌生的环境下也是如此。我很珍惜与世界各地的人们交流的机会。不利的方面是，国际化使我跟一辈子生活在同一个地方的人相比，缺少对某个地方的归属感。

50
人生之旅的镜像

I believe a person's strengths are reflected in their accomplishments and in the path they have followed from where they began in life to where they have arrived.

I think adaptability and flexibility are important strengths I developed. I grew up in a rather humble family and following work forced us to move all around Brazil. I was born in the poor northeast of Brazil, lived in the far north and spent my adolescence in the developed southeast. Befriending people from various economic and social backgrounds and always being ready to pack up and leave has forced me to develop a great deal of flexibility, making me ready to face adversity and change, to adapt to ever-changing situations and to deal with various cultures and values.

Another important strength that I believe my achievements reflect is determination. Throughout my life, I have had rewarding experiences, such as when I was an intern at Exxon during my senior year in college. The company was located sixty miles away and every Thursday I had to wake up at 4:30 A.M. and take three different bus rides before making it to Exxon in order to start working at 8:00 A.M. After working all day and spending the night in a youth hostel, I would repeat the drudgery on Friday and only make it back home at 11:00 at night. All of this while facing a tough curriculum in the most demanding engineering school in the country. The experience taught me the value of effort and commitment, not to mention it boosted my confidence when it came to facing the challenges the future held.

My main weakness is that I still focus too much on details. At a consulting company, learning to apply the "80/20" rule is critical to a successful project leader. By focusing on details, I end up misplacing my efforts and spending valuable time on details that will not add to my intuition and judgment. Although such ability comes with experience, I think two years of real-life case discussions at Harvard can guarantee the development of such qualities while shortening the time it would take should I wait to simply attain them on my own.

Another weakness that I have been working on a lot is assertiveness. I still need to be more effective in defending ideas and getting my point across in the presence of senior management. Although I feel I have improved a lot since I first joined BCG as an untried engineer, I am conscious that I still have a way to go in order to get where I want.

点评

本篇 Essay 很好地阐释了申请人应如何表达真诚的品质和雄心壮志。申请人用开头两段话阐明了自己因为出身卑微，所以他的优势是独一无二的。通过描述他从童年到 BCG 的道路并非一帆风顺，使读者可以了解他的个人发展和职业发展的重要性。申请人的写作风格直截了当、生动形象，轻松地呈现了他的经历。

申请人没有试图博取读者的同情心，而是真诚地分享了出生在一个贫寒的家庭、自幼四海为家、大学时往返数小时去实习这样一幅生活情景。这些小片段使得他的优势具有生气，同时也凸显了申请人多姿多彩的经历。随意且真诚的笔调彰显出申请人随和、容易亲近人的性格特征，与此同时，本篇 Essay 明确传达出他是一个兢兢业业、雄心勃勃、非常成功的人。

申请人指出了两项具体的缺点。这两项缺点都属于个人发展领域，且因为咨询公司的背景而成了他的缺点，但它们显示了申请人真诚的自我认知。而且，申请人漂亮地提到，加入哈佛商学院有助于他在这些方面的提升。事实上，他的缺点使他成为一名实力更强劲的申请人。

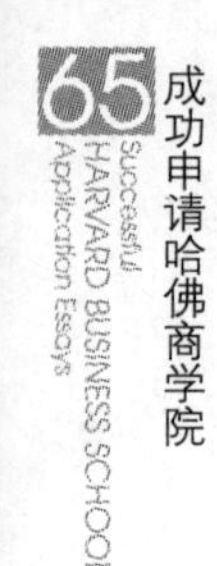

【参考译文】

我相信，一个人的优点是可以从他的成就、他的人生之旅中反映出来的。

我认为，适应性和灵活性是我具备的两大重要优点。我出生在一个贫寒的家庭，为了工作我们被迫奔波，走遍了整个巴西。我在贫穷的巴西东北部出生，在遥远的北方长大，又在发达的东南部度过了我的青春时光。与来自不同经济社会背景的人交朋友，随时准备收拾行囊上路，这些经历赋予了我极大的灵活性，让我随时准备面对逆境和变化，以适应不断变化的情况，应付各种不同的文化和价值观。

我相信，我的成就反映出的另一项优点是我具有坚定的决心。回顾我的生活，我有过一些颇有价值的经历。比如大四那年，我在埃克森美孚石油公司做实习生。公司离我的住所有 100 多千米远，每周四，我凌晨 4 点半就得起床，换乘三辆公交车，才能在早上 8 点之前赶到公司。工作了一天之后在青年旅馆凑合一晚，星期五继续这份苦差事，然后要到晚上 11 点才能到家。与此同时，我还要面对全国要求最苛刻的工程学校的困难课程。这段经历教会了我努力和承诺的价值，更不必说它增强了我在未来面临挑战时的自信心。

我的缺点是过于注重细节。在一家咨询公司，学习应用“80/20”法则是我成功胜任项目领导职责的关键。由于注重细节，我将自己的精力放错了地方，把宝贵的时间浪费在对我的直觉和判断无益的细节上。虽然这样的能力来源于经验，但我认为，哈佛商学院两年的实际案例探讨，能帮我提高这种品质，并缩短单靠我自己去掌握它们所需的时间。

我一直在努力改正的另一个缺点是武断。我还需要更有效地在高层管理人员面前为自己的想法辩护、传达自己的观点。虽然我感觉，自加入 BCG 公司以来，我作为一个无经验的工程师在这一点上已经有了很大的提高，但我意识到，为了达到目标，我还有很长的一段路要走。

51
寻找感情和商业敏锐性之间的平衡点

Two of my greatest strengths are (1) my ability to grasp the "big picture" and (2) my initiative—particularly in adding value to the institutions or environments in which I have interacted. I always scrutinize an opportunity to determine if other possibilities exist and if there is a way to grow the opportunity past its current level.

For example, I trained a government client on a financial and operational model that I had developed. During these sessions, I seized the opportunity to listen to the client's needs outside of the project's scope. In fact, one of the senior executives was so impressed with the quality of work and my genuine concern that she wanted to allocate her extra budget to another project for Booz Allen to further improve the client's operations. I took the idea to a principal and, as a result, my initiative led to work extensions for the firm.

My holistic, entrepreneurial perspective also extended to the community. In New York and Atlanta, I have organized several clothing and food drives for South Africa and Ghana and have sought individuals and groups to join these efforts. What was the big picture? For some, these drives represented the first opportunity to become involved in a foreign community service-project and thus introduced them to a simple way to give back.

My greatest weakness is my emotional involvement with my work. Oftentimes, clients expect recommendations, based on sound analysis, regardless of the implications. For one client, my team and I had to offer analytically driven recommendations to a client based on a congressional mandate. However, based on client interviews, I knew that many of these client members were not ready to assume some of the responsibilities inherent in our recommendations. Therefore, I struggled with my expectation that they would have to learn how to "walk before they crawled." On my current project, I am working on a post-merger integration project of two agribusiness clients. This is my first project in which possible layoffs and plant closings, due to excess workforces, may be an issue. Ever since our initial discussion of these options, I have had difficulty responding to the likelihood of people losing their jobs. At times, I have had to remind myself that my job involves providing objective recommendations without any emotional involvement. Otherwise, my emotion may cloud my judgment. However, I am aggressively thinking of ways to care for the client and also provide logical, sound business solutions. With counsel and experience, though, I am finding the true balance between my emotions and business acuity.

点 评

申请人通过两件事有效地表现了自己的两大优点。他清晰地阐述了这些个性如何交织在工作和生活中。此外，他列举的例子另有好处。这些例子含蓄地反映出申请人身上的其他优点，比如有效的沟通能力、单独与高层打交道的能力，以及带领一群人追求共同目标的能力。从这些例子可以看出，申请人是一个全面发展的人。

文章用一半的篇幅共两个事例来表现申请人最大的弱点——工作中感情用事。由于申请人非常诚实，具体解释了这种个性如何影响他的工作，所以这段自我批评收到了很好的效果。他意识到这个弱点在将来很可能会影响他的发展，这种认识体现出他的成熟和深谋远虑。申请人提到，他通过聆听其他人的忠告寻找适当的平衡点，这是针对目标改掉缺点的关键。

【参考译文】

我的两大优点分别是：把握全局和主动性——特别是主动为组织和所处的环境增加价值。我总是仔细审视每一个机会，判断是否还存在其他可能性，是否还有别的方法可以为机会增值。

例如，我曾为一家政府机构客户培训，讲解如何操作我开发的财务运算模型。培训期间，我把握机会，听取客户在此项目之外的其他需求。实际上，其中一位高管对我的工作品质以及我对项目发自内心的关心印象深刻，于是，他打算把额外的预算拨给博思艾伦公司的另一个项目，以便进一步改善业务。我把这个想法传达给一位负责人，结果是，我的主动性延长了与这家公司的合作时间。

我还将我的全局观和开创精神发展到社区的公益事业上。在纽约和亚特兰大，我为南非和加纳组织了几次捐赠衣服和食品的活动，并邀请到了众多个人和机构参与到此活动中来。该活动的宏观意义是什么呢？对有些人来说，这是他们第一次有机会参与国外的公益服务项目，也就是说，我向他们介绍了一条回馈社会的简单途径。

我最大的弱点是在工作中感情用事。通常情况下，客户期望我们基于正确的分析提出建议而不管可能产生的影响。根据委员会的要求，我所在的团队应该给一位客户提供带有分析性的建议书。然而，根据客户的访谈结果，我知道客户并不准备承担建议书中的一些责任。因此，我很犹豫，他们可能要在“学会爬之前走路”。眼下，我在处理两家农场客户合并之后的整合项目。这是我第一次处理这样的项目。由于劳动力过剩，可能会导致工厂关门、裁员。从第一次讨论执行方案起，我就难以正视有人可能会失业这个问题。我不得不时时提醒自己，我的工作需要提供客观的建议，不能受情感的影响，不然会混淆我的判断。但是，我正在积极想办法，试图找到既安置好客户又合乎逻辑的完美的商业解决方案。不过，随着自身经验的增长，通过咨询他人的建议，我正在寻找感情和商业敏锐性之间的平衡点。

52
一个自由职业者的激烈竞争生活

My main strengths include being both academically able and intellectually curious. I have proved myself to be as strong in economics as I am in English literature, mirrored in my work by an ability to read statistics and scripts with equal ease. In study, not only can I master the finer points of perfect competition and postcolonial literature, but I also come alive around these subjects. In the classroom at the London School of Economics, I argue with more passion, compassion, and insight than the aggregate of all my classmates.

In the real world, filming on the streets of the Bronx, I developed a skill base far removed from the one I had acquired within the ivory towers of academia. I was able to adapt instantly to ever-changing, challenging, and sometimes hostile situations. These circumstances facilitated my development into a strong leader who could guide others under the most testing circumstances. Working with film crews comprised of a hundred people—from the director to the driver—also taught me how to operate effectively as part of an incredibly diverse team.

Survival in a competitive freelance environment depends not only on how well you do, but also on how well you relate to people. I am simultaneously able to accomplish results and develop lasting working relationships. I communicate very clearly and problem-solve quickly and objectively. Through these strengths I have developed into a skilled negotiator and I am increasingly working in a deal-making capacity.

I am prepared to take risks and embrace new challenges; in choosing to work in film I took an uncertain course and, in the spirit of entrepreneurship, set up a company in a foreign country. I possess an extremely broad worldview; I have traveled and worked in many different environments and through the arts and my MBA I seek to further expand my outlook.

As in many cases, my flaws are bound up in my virtues. I am extremely determined, and if I set myself a course of action I will follow it to the very end. However, underlying this is a difficulty to stop fighting for an outcome which does not merit the time and energy invested in it. In teamwork situations I can find it difficult to engage with those who do not share my enthusiasm and commitment to a project. I can sometimes be tactless when conveying my opinions but with time I am learning to be more sensitive.

点评

简单地罗列自己的优势并不会使Essay更出彩。不过，申请人采用了具体的经历，聪明地把自己描绘成一个富有成效且充满活力的领导者。申请人深知，仅有学术成就不足以造就一名合格的经理人，于是她还展示了一系列更具实效的商业技能：灵活性、问题解决能力和沟通技能。

在本篇Essay中，申请人留给我们一个持久的印象：一位颇为自知的女性，精通经济学和文学，在电影制作工作中磨炼了她的领导才能，并敢于冒风险在异国他乡创办公司。多姿多彩的经历使她成为一名有意思的哈佛商学院候选人，同时，她知道如何在不同的环境下发挥自己优势，这表明她对管理拥有深刻的认知。

最后讲述缺点这一段似乎有点简短，尤其考虑到申请人用了大量的篇幅来阐述自己的优势。尽管如此，申请人还是十分具体地指出了自己有待提高的方面。没有试图用优势来代替缺点，而且她决心要在今后的日子里加以改进。这种就事论事的处理方法，也许正是她注重实效、目标明确的个性的另一种表现。

【参考译文】

我的主要优势包括学术能力和求知欲。我已经证明了自己在经济学和英国文学方面具有同样的实力，体现在工作中的表现就是，我能够同样轻松地阅读统计报告和文稿。在学业上，我不仅能够掌握自由竞争时期和后殖民时期文学的精妙之处，还能够做到活学活用。在伦敦经济学院的课堂上，我在辩论中表现出来的热情、同情心和洞见比所有同学的总和都要多。

在现实生活中，我在布朗克斯的街道上拍电影的经历，使我发展出一套与在学术象牙塔里掌握的截然不同的技能。我能够迅速适应不断变化的、艰难的，甚至有时是怀有敌意的环境。这些环境把我塑造成一名坚强的领导者，能够在最艰苦的形势下带领他人。与 100 名工作人员（从导演到司机）组成的电影摄制组一起工作，还教会了我如何在一个成员迥异的团队里有效工作。

想要在竞争激烈的自由职业者的环境下生存，不仅取决于你的工作是否出色，还要看你的人际交往能力如何。我能够在完成工作的同时与他人建立持久的工作关系。我与他人的沟通清晰而明确，解决问题迅速而客观。利用这些优势，我已经发展成了一名谈判专家，达成交易的能力也在日渐提高。

我做好了承担风险和迎接新挑战的准备。选择进入电影业，就意味着我走上了一条不确定的道路。在创业激情的鼓舞下，我在异国他乡创办了一家公司。我拥有十分开阔的世界观，曾在很多国家旅行和工作过，我希望凭借自己的文学素养及 MBA 的背景，进一步拓宽我的视野。

正如很多人一样，我的缺点与我的优势也是紧密相关的。我的性格极其坚定，一旦我给自己订下了一条行动路线，我必定沿着它走到底。然而，这背后的问题是，对于不值得投入时间和精力的事情，我也难以放手。在团队工作中，我发现自己很难与那些不能同我一样热情且无法为项目承担责任的人共事。有时，我在表达自己的观点时不够老练，不过随着年龄的增长，我正学着变得更加敏锐。

53
我是一个坦诚的人

In order to better convey who I am, I would like to detail three strong character traits that I believe stand out in my personality: *initiative, maturity,* and *open-mindedness.* There are also two areas—*communications* and *attention to detail*—which I have had the opportunity to improve over the past years. My challenge going forward is to improve my communications skills and to be more detailed without compromising the pace of my initiative or the drive to get things done.

People who know me tend to point out my *intellectual curiosity* and *initiative* as my most distinctive traits. These characteristics are the result of the environment where I was brought up, where commitment to hard work and ideals were considered key to achieve success. I have incorporated these thoughts and became eager to implement the ideas I found important.

Maturity is another strong element of my personality. However, this essential ingredient of a decision-maker did not come easily for me. Two years before completing high school, my parents got divorced and, as the oldest of four children, I often had to step into a parental role. This was probably the most difficult phase of my life. I came out of those times more responsible, mature in judgment, and more certain of what I wanted.

The other fundamental trait of my personality is my *open-mindedness*. I have always been very tolerant toward other cultures and interested in understanding different perspectives. That is why I have traveled a lot and tried to get to know different people from different cultures. While at university, I applied to spend a full year in Barcelona in an exchange program. It was one of the best years of my life. I also

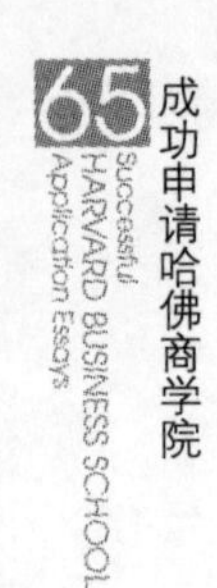

decided to visit Eastern European countries and Russia, be in places like Auschwitz or experience the liberal atmosphere of the Netherlands. I believe this transformed me into a more autonomous thinker and conscious person.

The last two years at McKinsey have helped me overcome some of my weaknesses, like *oral communication* and *attention to detail*. I actually only became aware of these limitations as I had to convey my messages to senior executives. I realized I had trouble tailoring the message to the audience, as well as summing up messages with complex and serious implications. I also recognized that my drive led me to sometimes overlook detail, which is essential to ensure the full accuracy of the content. Fortunately, I have had exposure to great mentors and plenty of opportunities to work on these aspects. Feedback that I have received shows me that I have made tangible progress.

点评

申请人在介绍优点的段落中解释了他为什么能够在哈佛商学院表现出色。他是一个努力、成熟、具有开放心态的人，也可能是一个会在哈佛商学院这种多元化的地方表现不俗的人（这一点是合乎逻辑的）。介绍缺点的部分非常诚实，但有点危险。比如，很少有申请人会承认自己口头交流有障碍，不过这并不是说所有哈佛商学院的申请人都擅长演讲（因为许多人在刚进学校时并不突出）。但是申请人的缺点依然有风险，因为哈佛的案例教学法要求学生能够向一群人自如地发表观点，并且，在面对可能持有不同意见的听众时捍卫你的观点。坦承自己不擅此道，就等于说你可能无法融入哈佛商学院教学的核心内容。当然，反过来就是，像申请人这样的人正应该上哈佛商学院，因为他将从中受益最多（鉴于学校强调公共演讲）。既然申请人已经顺利被哈佛商学院录取，我们能从中看出，诚实很少会伤害自己。

如果申请人在结尾举一个具体的例子，表现自己如何克服了那些缺点，那么，整篇文章将会更加令人满意。例如，给一位充满敌意的客户进行一次成功的演示。这样的故事比含糊地说一句“我已取得了显著的进步”更有意义。任何时候，只要有可能，就要用事实说话。不要光说你改进了，而是要给出你如何改进的例子。做到了这一点，你的文章看起来就会更加真实。本文由于申请人非常坦诚地告知自己的缺点，所以很少有人会怀疑他的诚恳。实际上，唯一的不足是我们想知道更多的情况。

【参考译文】

为了更好地展现我是怎样的人，我想详细介绍三个自认为最突出的性格优势：主动、成熟和开放的心态。还有两处我有幸在过去几年得以改善的地方——沟通和关注细节。我面临的挑战是，在不影响主动性和行动力的前提下，提高沟通技巧和关注细节的能力。

认识我的人通常认为求知欲强和积极主动是我最突出的优点。我成长的环境造就了这些个性特征。在我生长的地方，人们相信努力工作和追逐梦想是成功的关键。我深受这种思维的影响，渴望把我认为重要的想法付诸实践。

个性成熟是我的又一个优点。然而，这项决策者必备的素质对我而言并非与生俱来。高中毕业前两年，我的父母离婚了。作为4个子女中最年长的一个，我经常需要扮演家长的角色。这可能是我一生中最艰苦的阶段。熬过了那段时光，我变得更加富有责任心，对事情的评价更加中肯，也更清楚我想要的是什么。

第三个优点是我拥有开放的心态。我对其他文化非常包容，乐于接受不同的观点，这就是我为什么走南闯北想要结交许多不同文化背景的人的原因。大学时，我申请去巴塞罗那做一年的交换生。那段经历是我生命中最美好的时光之一。我还决定要去东欧国家和俄罗斯走一走，感受一下奥斯威辛集中营这样的地方，或者去体会一下荷兰那种自由散漫的氛围。我相信，这能使我成为一个更具独立思考意识的有自知之明的人。

过去两年，在麦肯锡工作的经历帮助我克服了一些缺点，比如口头沟通上的障碍以及对细节缺乏关注能力。实际上，我在不得不向高层汇报工作时才意识到这些缺点。我发现自己不懂得如何根据听众剪裁信息，以及不知道如何对复杂的有重要影响的信息作总结、归纳。我也承认，我的冲劲有时使我忽略细节，而细节是确保内容完整、准确的根本。幸运的是，我接触到一些伟大的导师，让我有足够的机会提升、改进。从我得到的反馈来看，我已经取得了显著的进步。

WHY DO YOU NEED AN HBS MBA?

命题 8
我为什么选择哈佛商学院

Why do you wish to pursue an MBA degree from Harvard Business School? What are your career aspirations and why?

What are your career aspirations, and how can Harvard Business School help you to reach them?

你为什么希望来哈佛商学院进修 MBA 学位？你的职业追求是什么？原因何在？

你的职业追求是什么？哈佛商学院可以怎样帮助你实现你的追求？

解题思路

你已经出色地回答了其他几个命题，但是，你知道自己毕业后想要什么吗？你为你的事业制订了长远的目标吗？你现在真的需要一个 MBA 学位吗？为什么要来哈佛商学院拿这个学位呢？

这个看似简单的问题，也许是所有 Essay 命题中最重要的一个问题，也可能是最具挑战性的一个问题了。你以为你知道答案，或者说，你以为你应该知道，可是当你坐下写 Essay 的时候，你会发现很难表达清楚自己的职业计划，以及 MBA 学位在整个计划中处于怎样的位置。刚开始时的艰难并不意味着你还没准备好读一个 MBA 学位，也不意味着你不是哈佛商学院的出色候选人。这个命题涉及一个核心问题，即你是怎样的一个人，你在生活中想要达到哪些目标？这些问题都很难解决，也很难说清楚。

下笔的时候，要先确定你已经理解了自己的宏伟计划——你想如何塑造你自己以及你周围的世界？思考下列问题可以帮助你构思你的宏图：什么东西能给我带来快乐？我的优点和缺点是什么？我最重要的价值又是什么？先写另外五篇 Essay 会有助于你集中精神思考这些问题。能够定义你这个人的驱动力是什么？这是此类命题成功的基础。否则，你的文章会显得千篇一律，毫无激情。

请试着按下列步骤来组织你的思路，不过行文没必要局限于此。

第一，将你现有的经历放入你的宏图伟业中，特别要阐明它们与你未来的目标有何相关。第二，制订近期和长期的职业计划。这些计划应该是现实可行的，并且是基于你的经历和个人兴趣的。考虑一下你想如何影响这个社会，然后将其分解成达成目标的不同阶段。第三，评估你的经历与目标的距离，明确 MBA 课程可以如何弥补这段距离。第四，判断哈佛商学院的哪些特殊之处适合你的目标，并将你的职业抱负与学校的使命联系起来，然后再想想你能对 MBA 课程作何贡献。

本部分挑选的范文包含了上述所有或大多数要素。虽然它们没有直接说明，但都传达出了一种个人远见与职业抱负紧密相连的一致性。虽然其写作风格和内容截然不同，但所有这些 Essay 都在探索申请人的职业道路——它们作为变化的媒介将满足申请人的雄心，并且展示了哈佛商学院将如何提供转变经验，帮助他们达成目标。

点评人： 萨拉·切尔林（Sara Cherlin）

54
投身私募基金行业

Throughout my professional career, I have experienced the mergers and acquisitions process from a number of different perspectives— investment banking, private equity, incubator/accelerator, and real estate management. Each of these opportunities has enabled me to build upon my transactional skills and develop a strong financial background. After almost six years of deal-related experience in various industries I have decided to pursue a career in private equity, with the ultimate goal of becoming a managing partner at a private equity fund. My past work experiences have prepared me with the practical know-how and quantitative skills to prosper in this field. Nonetheless, I must gain more exposure to marketing and strategic management issues in order to accomplish my short- and long-term career goals.

An MBA education from the Harvard Business School will provide me with superior management skills and a greater level of business sophistication. Harvard's innovative curriculum, as well as its emphasis on entrepreneurship and the case method, will expose me to the intricacies of negotiation as well as entrepreneurial and strategic management. By working with a diverse group of professionals in study groups and team projects, I will become familiar with foreign business practices and techniques. The lively discussions and seminars given by CEOs of *Fortune* 500 companies will introduce me to the personal qualities inherent in an outstanding senior-level manager. In my future career as a managing partner of a private equity fund, I will, undoubtedly, hold several board positions in portfolio companies, so a solid background in corporate strategy will be essential to my professional goals.

Clearly, a Harvard MBA education will offer me the analytical skills, the teamwork and leadership instincts, and the business savvy to succeed in the private equity sector. At HBS, I will mature into a well-rounded business professional, building long-lasting relationships with my colleagues and taking advantage of Harvard's exceptional business resources.

点 评

本篇 Essay 内容紧凑、结构严谨，清晰地表达了申请人希望进入哈佛商学院的强烈欲望。申请人具体记叙了他从商学院毕业后打算做的事情（升迁为一名私募基金公司的任事股东），以及为达到目标（市场营销及企业战略）需要学习的知识。申请人还点出了对于私募经理来说或许是最关键的任务，即评估投资组合公司中的那些 CEO 和高层经理，这一点做得非常漂亮。他提出的理由是，在哈佛商学院，他会遇见这些未来的公司领袖，并且了解他们的驱动力和成功的原因。本篇 Essay 唯一的不足是，申请人没有强调他能为哈佛商学院带来什么，以及他会为这个社群作出什么贡献。在如此短的篇幅中，你必须有所取舍，但一两句有关这方面的话能为文章带来进一步的升华。不过，这依然是一篇瑕不掩瑜的好范文！

【参考译文】

在我的整个职业生涯中，我从许多不同的角度经历了公司的兼并和收购过程——投资银行、私募基金、企业孵化器以及房产管理公司。每一个机会都帮助我提升了业务处理技能，并为我打下了坚实的金融背景。在不同行业从事了大约 6 年的交易工作后，我决定在私募基金行业追求自己的事业，最终目标是在一家私募基金公司里担任经营合伙人。我之前的工作经历使我具备了在该行业成功所必需的实际知识和定量分析技术。但是，为了实现我的短期及长期事业目标，我必须更多地了解市场营销及战略管理问题。

哈佛商学院的 MBA 教育能给我带来出众的管理技能以及更高水平的商务经验。哈佛的创新课程，以及对创业精神和案例分析教学法的强调，将使我了解到商务谈判与企业战略管理的复杂性。通过在学习小组和团队项目中与不同的专业人士合作，我会熟悉其他国家的商业惯例和技巧。由《财富》500强企业的CEO主持的生动讨论及研讨会，将使我了解杰出高层管理人员的内在个人品质。在未来我作为私募基金公司经营合伙人的工作中，无疑需要担任一些投资组合公司的董事职位，因而在企业战略方面的扎实背景对于我的职业目标是必不可少的。

显然，哈佛的MBA教育会培养我的分析技能、团队合作技能和领导技能，以及在私募公司获得成功所需的商业头脑。在哈佛商学院，我会利用非凡的商业资源成长为一名全面的商界人士，与同僚建立持久的关系。

55 管理多元化资源公司

My long-term goal is to be a leader in the energy business of a diversified resources company such as Rio Tinto, because such a position would enable me to make a positive contribution to some of the important challenges—global consolidation, for example—facing the resource industry.

While my operational experience will be invaluable in achieving this goal, I require specific skills that will not be acquired on mine sites. Instead, formal training in finance, general management, and international business will be required. HBS courses such as Leading Change and Organizational Renewal and Managing International Trade and Investment will provide these skills.

HBS is the best environment in which to acquire these skills for three reasons:

Working on real business problems as an analyst taught me a great deal about business in general. This indicates that the case-study method used by Harvard would be an extremely effective way to acquire the mind-set necessary to achieve my career goals.

Addressing the challenges faced by the resource industry effectively will require empathy with decision-makers in a wide range of roles—financial, regulatory, customers, and competitors. Working closely with other students—given their diverse interests and experiences—would help me develop this empathy. At the same time, I feel my unusual professional experiences and interests would be a valuable contribution to the HBS community.

The problems faced by the resource industry require a global view. The global focus of HBS's curriculum, and the broad backgrounds of its students, would provide an excellent environment in which to meet this requirement.

After graduation, I intend to join the business development group of a diversified resources company. In such a role, a global view is crucial in identifying the commercial opportunities available in the resource industry, and to assess the implications of those opportunities. The specific skills acquired at HBS would allow me to maximize the value of those opportunities.

点评

申请人对于毕业后希望干什么非常明确，并且解释了为什么继续工作无法达成目标（例如在煤矿，他无法接触到财务或者综合管理方面的培训），这往往有利于解释为什么非进商学院不可。申请人在文中给出的解释非常充分。

除此之外，本文的可信度来自于申请人对哈佛商学院的深入了解。显然，他事先做过调查，仿佛曾亲临气氛活跃的课堂讨论现场一般。他还意识到，鉴于他那非典型的工作背景，给哈佛商学院带去的好处同商学院能提供给他的收获一样多。在此强调这一点是申请人正确的选择，对于你能为学校带来的贡献，要直接说出来，别犹豫。并不是说你应该吹嘘，但是，你确实需要提出有利的论据，表明如果哈佛商学院录取你将能获得什么益处。由于本文的情况特殊，申请人甚至可以更进一步，具体描述一下他的“特殊专业经验和兴趣爱好”可以为哈佛带来什么。

【参考译文】

我的长期目标是管理一家多元化的资源公司，比如力拓公司。我的理由是，作为一名管理者，我可以为资源产业面临的重大挑战，比如全球性资源整合，作出积极贡献。

虽然拥有实际操作经验对于实现我的目标来说非常宝贵，但我也需要一些在矿场学不到的具体技能，而财务、综合管理、国际商务方面的正规培训是必需的。哈佛商学院的课程中，比如领导组织变革和更新以及国际贸易投资管理就训练这些技能。

哈佛商学院是学习这些技能的最佳场所，原因有三：

第一，作为分析师，我在解决真正的商业问题时，学到了大量的商业知识。这表明，哈佛使用的案例研究法是非常有效的学习方式，能帮我掌握实现目标所需的思考模式。

第二，要想有效解决能源行业面临的挑战，需要以一系列广泛的决策者的角色（金融、管理、客户和竞争对手）引起共鸣。与拥有不同兴趣和经验的同学一起学习，会提高我的共情能力。同时，我也相信自己特殊的专业经历和兴趣爱好将成为哈佛商学院课堂的宝贵财富。

第三，资源产业面临的问题需要全球化的观点才能解决。哈佛商学院着眼于全球的课程体系以及学生们的广阔背景，它可以为我提供一个良好的环境，训练我的全球化观点。

毕业后，我打算加入一家多元化资源公司的业务发展部门。从事这一行，拥有全球性的视野，在识别有利于资源产业发展的商业机会和评估这些机会的影响上至关重要。哈佛商学院要求的这些技能有利于我将这些机会所创造的价值最大化。

56
创建全球化品牌公司

By working in the consumer goods, retail, and e-tail practices at McKinsey, I explored the option of turning a childhood love for branded products into a full-blown career. Moving to Ethcentric, I dug deeper into these prospects and began to focus on how companies connect with their consumers through target marketing. From these experiences, I've learned that companies create products that reflect their perspectives of consumers' everyday lives, while people purchase specific products to exhibit their own view of their lifestyles. Combining this insight with my professional and personal experiences, I realize my professional goal is to create a global branded products company that will improve the self-images of ethnic communities by promoting the most wonderful aspects of each culture in its product marketing.

To do this, I'll need the most rigorous general management training applicable across multiple platforms, the strongest network to leverage as my business develops and the most renowned credentials for the capital markets. Firstly, Harvard's unique case method approach will elevate my ability to make sound decisions with limited information. My diverse professional experiences in research and development, plant operations, retail operations, mergers and acquisitions, interactive marketing, and grassroots campaigning have taught me that complete information never exists. Secondly, the HBS experience will provide me with a global network of leaders on which to call as my business grows from a regional start-up to a national conglomerate to an international vehicle for cultural appreciation. By taking leadership roles in the African-American Student Union, the most influential African-American alumni network in the world, and the Retail and Apparel Club, a rare gem exclusive to HBS among top general management programs, I will develop lasting relationships with world leaders. Finally, I will need to raise capital to grow this business. The credibility gained with a Harvard MBA will drive discussions with potential investors quickly beyond my management capabilities to the execution of my ideas.

As I consider the tools I need to achieve my professional goals, the Harvard Business School is the only place for me to get them all. I can't wait to start!

点评

本篇 Essay 清晰地描写了哈佛商学院的 MBA 学位可以如何帮助申请人达成目标，同时又传达出申请人的热情。他从一开始就摆出了过去的相关经历，然后又清晰地说明这些经历如何引导他认识自己的长期职业目标。由于他过去在产品和营销方面的经历，他想在生活消费品领域有所成就的愿望显得非常现实。另外，积极参与美籍非裔学生会的经历，也证实了他献身种族团体的承诺。

通过叙述美籍非裔学生会及其他学生俱乐部的经历，申请人有力地说明了为什么哈佛商学院的课程特别适合他，以及他如何计划在校园内担任领导角色。虽然对案例分析教学法和强大的关系网这方面的评论不算新鲜（并不需要句句都新颖），但仍然证明了申请人曾全盘考虑过哈佛 MBA 的课程，所有这些方面都明显与他的创业目标联系在一起。总体来说，申请人基于自身的经历和计划，展示了明确的方向和目标。结尾的最后一句与整篇 Essay 的基调相互印证，并传达出申请人真正的热情。

【参考译文】

通过我在麦肯锡公司从事消费品、零售及电子商务等方面的业务，我发现可以将幼年对品牌产品的热爱转化成一个全盛的事业。进入 Ethcentric 公司后，我更加深入地挖掘这些业务的前景，并开始聚焦于公司如何通过目标市场营销与消费者建立联系。从这些经历中，我认识到，公司开发的产品体现了他们对消费者日常生活的认知，而人们购买特定产品反映了他们对生活方式的想法。

结合我的个人职场经历与这条洞见，我意识到，我的职业目标是创建一家全球化的品牌产品公司，利用产品营销活动，推广产品代表的那种文化的精华，从而改善种族群体的自我形象。

为了达到这个目标，我需要接受最严格的适用于多种平台的综合管理训练，还需要支持我的公司发展的最强有力的关系网，以及在资本市场上最有声誉的信任度。第一，哈佛独特的案例分析教学法可以提升我根据有限信息作出明智决策的能力。我在研究与开发、工厂运作、零售业务、兼并与收购、互动式营销以及基层营销活动等方面，有着多样化的职业经历，这些经历使我明白，我永远不可能得到全面的信息。第二，在哈佛商学院就读的经历可以为我编织一张全球商界领袖的关系网，凭借这张关系网，我可以使公司从一个区域性的初创企业发展成全国性的联合企业，再到具有文化品位的国际化公司。通过在美籍非裔学生会（全球最有影响力的美籍非裔校友网）和零售与服装俱乐部（哈佛唯一拥有的顶级综合管理组织中的佼佼者）担任领导，我将与全球商界领袖建立持久的关系。第三，我需要筹集资本，发展公司。一个哈佛 MBA 的可信度，将推进我与潜在投资者之间的讨论，迅速超越我的自我管理能力，实现我的计划。

在我考虑实现自己的职业目标所需的各种工具时，只有哈佛商学院能帮我全部实现。我已经迫不及待了！

57
成为福特分公司总裁

My career aspirations are twofold:

First, become president of a Ford subsidiary in South America (i.e., Ford Argentina, Chile or Venezuela).

Second, increase the awareness of the benefits of diversity and socioeconomic development in the South American corporate sector by:

• Becoming a board member of a consultancy group that helps corporations leverage their internal diversity, develop effective corporate citizenship strategies, and find creative means to develop successful paradigms for corporate and social interaction.

• Establishing a continental award and grant program, funded by corporations, which recognizes individual, group, and corporate achievements to socioeconomic development.

Having gained leadership experiences in product development and operations across four continents and with a need for a strong foundation of general business skills, the HBS MBA becomes the essential stepping-stone to my career aspirations.

HBS will help me achieve my aspirations in the following ways:

Global problem-solving

I believe the HBS MBA will give me the skills and leadership thinking necessary to make the best decisions to resolve complex global problems. Through the HBS Latin American Research Center in Buenos Aires, I hope to conduct research with the

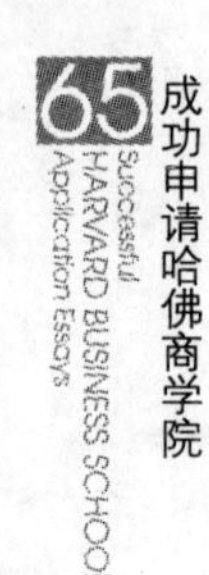

objective of developing a corporate strategy designed to increase profit and improve social conditions, as well as improve my business Spanish.

Dynamic Learning

After observing a study group and three HBS classes, I experienced a unique learning atmosphere of insight, diversity, and perspective and an atmosphere most compatible with my learning style. The interactive classroom participation, cold calls, and the case study learning method will give me the unique opportunity to engage, contribute, challenge, and be challenged by the perspectives and backgrounds of my classmates and faculty.

International credibility and a global network

The global reputation of HBS will be a critical vote of confidence that will ensure key international opportunities at levels where I can make an immediate impact and maintain my career path. Also, with the vast network of overseas HBS alumni, I will be able call upon skills, influence, and leadership to refine my vision, build corporate alliances, and establish friendships.

The total experience

My discussions with alumni have convinced me that HBS will give me an invaluable experience of learning, relationships, and enjoyment. This transforming experience will help me forge the character, courage, and confidence necessary to reach my professional and personal goals.

点 评

本文摒弃了传统的段落式写作格式而采用工作备忘录风格，这表明任何写作格式都同样有效。申请人生动地说明哈佛商学院的课程将如何引导他追求职业目标。信息表达前后一致，并且用了大量的有关哈佛商学院的细节加以佐证。显然，申请人事先做了充分的准备，对哈佛 MBA 课程以及哈佛商学院教育带来的更多收益表现出浓厚的兴趣。同前面几篇文章一样，申请人应当说明自己能为哈佛商学院带来什么好处，寥寥数语即可，这样一来说服力就会更强。申请人列出的细入毫芒的收益清单，表明申请人希望在加入哈佛商学院后收获的好处，如果相应列举一些他能为学校的学习环境所作的贡献，那么文章内容就均衡、对称了。

【参考译文】

我的职业抱负分为两方面：

第一，成为福特汽车公司南美分公司（比如，福特阿根廷、福特智利或福特委内瑞拉）的总裁。

第二，使南美的商业人士提升多元化收益和社会经济发展的意识，有如下几个手段：

· 加入一家顾问公司的董事会，致力于拓展企业内部的多样性，制订有效的企业公民战略，寻找创新的方式，以树立企业和社会互动的成功范例。

· 设立一个南美大陆奖励基金项目，由企业出资，表彰个人、团队和企业在社会经济发展方面的成就。

我曾在 4 个大洲带领过产品开发和运作的团队，拥有丰富的领导经验，同时渴望拥有综合商务技能的坚实基础，所以，加入哈佛商学院修 MBA 课程将是我实现职业抱负的不可或缺的阶梯。

哈佛商学院将在以下几个方面能助我实现理想。

全球性问题的解决能力

我相信，哈佛商学院的 MBA 课程将教我在面对复杂的全球性问题时所需要的技能和领导思维。通过设在布宜诺斯艾利斯的哈佛商学院拉美研究中心，我希望主持企业战略研究，旨在增加企业利润、改善社会条件，同时提高我的商务西班牙语能力。

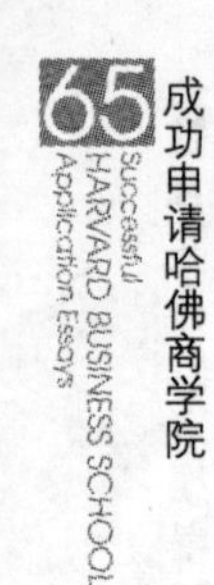

动态的学习方式

我在参观了一个研究小组又旁听了三堂 MBA 课程之后，感受到一种独特的学习氛围：睿智、多样、透彻，这非常符合我的学习风格。互动式的课堂教学、陌生电话以及案例研究学习法，给予我参与、贡献、挑战的独特机会，还可以与不同背景、不同观点的同学和老师进行辩论。

国际声誉和全球人际网络

哈佛商学院在国际上的声誉将成为我信心的关键来源，确保我在重要的国际组织里得到重要的工作机会，可以立刻发挥我的影响力，同时有助于我的职业发展。此外，我将拥有哈佛商学院庞大的校友关系网，可以利用他们的能力、影响力和领导力来开阔我的视野，建立企业联盟，同时结交朋友。

丰富的经历

与几位校友交谈之后，我深信哈佛商学院将是我生命中一段宝贵的经历：学习技能、建立友谊、享受生活。这段转型之旅有利于我塑造个性，增强勇气和信心，从而实现职业目标和个人追求。

58
帮助各国挖掘竞争优势

My career aspiration is to be a leader in economic development, particularly international economic development. I believe the best way to achieve a sustainable change in poverty is to create business opportunities and jobs in poor areas. Short term, I plan to work for organizations such as the United Nations, the World Bank, and foundations that influence growth in developing countries. In the long run, I plan to lead an international organization that helps countries identify their competitive advantages for business and sustainable development.

Through my past work experience, I have gained tremendous business skills and understanding of economic development theories. In my current role at ICIC, I am applying Professor Michael Porter's theories to help inner-city areas identify competitive advantages to attract businesses and create jobs for their residents. I would like to broaden the application of this economic development model to developing countries around the world. To do this successfully, I need to learn more about business strategy and how to manage large organizations, both core components of Harvard's MBA program.

Pursuing a degree from HBS will provide me the platform I need to achieve my career aspirations. In particular, the general management focus, the case method, and the Social Enterprise Initiative will prepare me to be an effective leader in economic development. First, the general management focus will provide me with the breadth of skills that I will need to lead and run an organization. Second, the case method will prepare me to deal with the challenges faced by leaders in making decisions with limited information. Finally, the classes and programs available through the

Social Enterprise Initiative will help me learn to lead in the social sector. Outside of the classroom, I plan to take a leadership role in organizations such as the Social Enterprise Club and the International Development Club so that I can network with students and faculty who share my interests.

I have visited HBS classes and was impressed by the diverse perspectives and the engaging discussions. I believe I will be an asset at HBS because I will contribute my passion for leveraging business in economic development, my experience in the for-profit and non-profit sectors, and my initiative both inside and outside the classroom. I look forward to being at HBS next year and am certain that I will be a valuable member of the community.

点评

本篇 Essay 给人留下了深刻的印象。申请人点到了这个命题的全部关键元素，而且言辞中肯、文字出彩。Essay 的开篇就为他的职业抱负定下了提纲挈领的"使命"，接着是十分具体的短期和长期目标，依据申请人的背景和兴趣，这些也显得非常现实。他还提到了几个组织的名字，使我们可以相信他确实做了深思熟虑的计划。

申请人也能清楚地说明自己为什么需要一个 MBA，而且是现在就需要。为了从一个以面向国内为主的职位转向一个全球性的工作，申请人想要在自己已经取得一些专门技能的领域（经济发展）拓展知识面。他很清楚哈佛商学院 MBA 项目的过人之处，并将其与自己的职业目标联系在了一起。

申请人提到他曾参观过哈佛商学院，还暗示他对课堂上的讨论很感兴趣由此可见他对这个项目的投入。他不仅表明这个项目可以给他带来的益处，还提到他可以如何反馈哈佛商学院，以及给这个学习环境带来什么，如此一来，他就把 Essay 提升了一个高度。本篇 Essay 非常有说服力，最终使得哈佛商学院的录取委员会心悦诚服地接收了申请人。

【参考译文】

我的职业抱负是成为一名经济发展领域的领导者，尤其是在国际经济发展领域。我相信，要想有效改善贫困，最好的方法是在贫困地区创造商业机会和就业机会。短期来看，我计划为联合国、世界银行等组织和影响发展中国家经济增长的基金会工作。长远来看，我计划领导一个国际组织，帮助各国挖掘它们在商业和可持续发展中的竞争优势。

在过去的工作经历中，我掌握了大量的商业技能，对经济发展理论有了一些理解。我目前在 ICIC 组织的工作就应用了迈克尔·波特教授的理论，帮助内地城市确立竞争优势，从而招商引资，为其居民创造就业机会。我希望把这个经济发展模型的应用扩大到全世界的发展中国家。为了能成功完成这一计划，我需要学习更多有关商业策略的知识以及管理大型组织的方法，两者都是哈佛 MBA 课程的核心内容。

哈佛商学院的 MBA 可以给我提供实现职业抱负所需的平台。其中，综合管理聚焦、案例分析教学法、社会事业创新等课程，将使我成为经济发展领域里的一名有效的领导者。首先，综合管理聚焦可以为我提供领导和管理一个组织所需的综合技能。其次，案例分析教学法可以使我应对在信息有限的情况下作决策所面临的挑战。最后，社会事业创新安排的课程和活动可以帮助我学习领导社会部门。课堂外，我的计划是在诸如社会事业俱乐部、国际发展俱乐部等社团里担任领导职务，从而让我可以与志同道合的同学和老师建立关系。

我曾参观过哈佛商学院，对课堂上形形色色的观点和引人入胜的讨论留下了深刻的印象。我相信，我会成为哈佛商学院的一份无形资产，因为我将贡献自己在经济发展中运用商业的热情、在盈利和非营利部门工作的经验，以及课内课外活动的主动性。我期待明年能进入哈佛商学院，且无疑会成为一名有价值的成员。

59
帮助外国企业打开日本市场

My immediate goal after getting an MBA is to continue working for a global consulting firm and to help foreign companies enter and excel in the Japanese market. Although most of the major American corporations have entered and built their presences in Japan a long time ago, there are many small- and medium-sized American companies who have no idea about their potential in the Japanese market or any international market. Yet there are few resources in Japan with enough industry expertise, communication skills, international network, and management skills to help. This is where I want to contribute.

To attain the most flexibility in multinational consulting, my long-term goal is to take over my father's business and expand it to offer more services. About fifteen years ago, my father launched CoTech International, Inc., which files and settles international intellectual property cases and runs a search database for Madrid Protocol, an international trademark protocol. I would like to combine the company's current service of intellectual property transactions and research with a consulting service to help clients enter foreign markets.

I am impressed with HBS's focus on developing global business leaders, analyzing successful businesses through case studies, and building an international student body. An HBS education will offer me an objective view of the characteristics of a successful business, by learning different cases of multinational businesses in an academic environment with a world-class faculty and state-of-the-art facilities. At the same time, I believe that my bicultural-bilingual background and experiences would be a great contribution to the school in creating an interesting and international student body. It may be too late to be a pioneer for large businesses in Japan, but with an HBS education under my belt, I can become a Japanese pioneer in expanding international business opportunities for small businesses.

点评

本文非常简洁、明了。申请人用两段精心写就的文字阐述了自己的长期目标和短期目标，接着叙述他将如何追求这些目标，增强了文章的说服力。申请人的目标看上去是一个很实际的过程。商学院毕业后又如此这般拓展父亲公司的业务范围，于是成功唾手可得，这个设想的过程合情合理。申请人想帮助小企业在日本成长，这个承诺贯穿全文直至结尾，一致性使文章显得更加真诚。他清晰地解释了为什么要在哈佛攻读 MBA，还强调了他为什么会成为哈佛商学院学生团体的一个有益补充，这一点让整篇文章无懈可击。

【参考译文】

我在修完 MBA 之后的近期目标是，继续为一家全球咨询公司工作，帮助外国公司进入日本市场，并且发挥优势。虽然许多美国大公司早早就进入了日本市场，且在日本民众心中树立了形象，但是仍有很多中小型美国企业不清楚他们在日本或其他国际市场的潜力。然而，日本可以利用的具备行业经验、沟通技巧、国际人脉网络、管理技能的资源十分有限，而这就是我想要一展拳脚的领域。

为了最大限度地发挥跨国咨询公司的灵活性，我的长远目标是接管父亲的公司并开拓公司的业务。大约 15 年前，父亲创立了 CoTech 国际公司，专门起诉国际知识产权案件，并解决相关的纠纷。父亲的公司还为《马德里议定书》（一个国际商标注册的系统）建立了可供检索的数据库。我想把公司现有的知识产权事务和研究与咨询服务结合起来，帮助客户打入国际市场。

哈佛商学院以培养全球商业领袖为重，以成功企业作为案例学习分析，致力于打造国际学生团体，这些都给我留下了深刻的印象。在一个学术环境里，利用先进的教学设备，与世界顶级的学者一起学习各种跨国企业案例，这样的哈佛商学院教育能让我客观地看待成功企业的特征。同时，我相信我的双语背景和多元文化体验将有利于学校打造有趣的国际学生团体。成为创立日本大企业的先驱可能为时已晚，但是，有了哈佛商学院的教育背景，我可以成为帮助小企业打开国际市场的日本先驱。

60

成就我的非营利性事业

"Harvard Business School? Are you kidding? It's too competitive! You're too young! Continue with your career. In two more years, you'll be making plenty of money." That is the reaction from my colleagues and friends when I tell them I am applying to business school.

Despite resistance from my peers, my desire to attend HBS could not be stronger. My short-term goal is to become a financial manager in the nonprofit sector with my long-term goal to found and lead my own foundation focused on inner-city development. Through my volunteer activities with St. Jude Children's Research Hospital, Habitat for Humanity, and Hands on Memphis, I have recognized a strong need for business managers in the nonprofit sector. After attending HBS, I aspire to lead an organization addresses the needs of underprivileged citizens in my community. Earning an MBA at this point in my life is a perfect choice, providing me with an opportunity to acquire the tools I need to begin a new chapter.

So what have I been up to in my career that has led to this realization? Quite surprisingly, I have been working as an investment banker for Morgan Keegan in what has been coined the "world of higher finance." Indeed, like many young, ambitious college graduates, I have been chasing the golden dream—BMW, limousines, three-story house, first-class service. Here we come, guns blazing! What is happening to me now? Did I suddenly develop a conscience, or did too many late nights at the office make me delusional and idealistic? No, I believe something else is finally had the courage to pursue what truly makes me happy, ignoring what is going to make me the most money or what my friends might think.

"But why nonprofit?" my coworkers jeer. "Are you going to be a social worker or go to Africa and live in a hut?" Absolutely not, my fiancee would kill me. But there are incredible opportunities to become part of social-enterprise initiatives at U.S. corporations or manage independent nonprofits. Historically, nonprofits have lacked savvy business managers. These entities need talented MBA graduates to help find creative solutions to challenges in the community. Harvard's social-enterprise program will enable me to explore issues in nonprofit management and to expand my business skills while providing me access to professional opportunities after graduation.

Community service has been a passionate part of my life, from my experiences mentoring at the Boys & Girls Club of Knoxville to my more recent involvement with Habitat for Humanity and Hands on Memphis. Through these leadership experiences, I have found something special in my life that I want to make an integral part of my career.

The case study method at HBS will be an invaluable opportunity to interact with students that have the same aspirations as I do. The diversity of the student body will enable me to see the world through different eyes, to broaden my perspective on how to approach different problems and to build a network of friendships that will last a lifetime. Through these types of experiences, I am confident I will make a meaningful impact on a nonprofit organization postgraduation.

点评

诚恳的语调及对话式的行文令本篇 Essay 脱颖而出。申请人清晰地表达了自己在非营利性组织工作的短期及长期目标，并列举出他投身社区的例子，充分地证实了他转换事业发展方向的目的。哈佛商学院为能参与申请人的转变而自豪，同时申请人也说明了他将如何大胆地利用这一优势。

最重要的是，在他最终鼓起勇气来权衡个人的雄心与他已经在走的“投行家之路”的时刻，他能明确地证明 MBA 学位为什么在现在对他如此重要。在投行工作的生活方式或许适合别人，不过申请人意识到，这显然不是他要追求的道路。为了完成这个转变，来哈佛商学院进修，包括他提到的通过社会事业课程学习非营利性组织的管理知识，将是一段非常宝贵的经历。

申请人的写作风格让读者跟着一起经历了一场灵魂探寻之旅，完成了事业上的选择。他不仅坦承了自己对事业的顿悟，也指出了他可能会遭遇的局限。这份直率恰恰证实了其计划的真实性。

【参考译文】

“哈佛商学院？你在开玩笑吗？竞争太激烈了！你还太年轻！继续干你现在的工作，再过两年，你就赚上大钱了！”这是同事和朋友听说我正在申请哈佛商学院之后的反应。

尽管同事们反对，但我想进入哈佛商学院的热情却无法熄灭。我的短期目标是在非营利性组织担任一名财务经理，而长期目标是创建并领导我自己的旨在发展内陆城市的基金会。通过我在圣·祖得儿童研究医院、国际仁人家园和Hands on Memphis等组织参加的义务活动，我了解到非营利性组织对商业经理的迫切需求。加入哈佛商学院之后，我渴望领导一个组织，专门解决我所在社区下层市民的需求。在我人生的这个时刻，获得一个MBA学位是一个完美的选择，可以给我一个机会去获取揭开人生新篇章所需的工具。

那么，是怎样的工作经历指引我去实现这个理想呢？令人惊讶的是，我曾在号称“顶级金融世界”的摩根·基根公司担任投资银行家。的确，像很多年纪轻轻而雄心勃勃的大学毕业生一样，我也曾追逐黄金梦——宝马车、豪华名车、三层别墅、一流的服务等，我曾为这些赴汤蹈火！那么，我现在又是怎么啦？突然之间良心发现啦？在办公室熬夜太多使我产生幻觉，变成理想主义者了？都不是。我终于有勇气去追求真正让我快乐的事业，无视那些最能挣钱的行业，将朋友们的看法置之度外。

“但是，为什么要选非营利性组织呢？”我的同事们讥讽道，“你打算当社工申请人吗？还是搬去非洲住木屋呢？”绝对不是，不然我的未婚妻会杀了我的。不过，成为美国公司的社会事业先驱，或者管理独立的非营利性组织，的确机会多多。从历史上来看，非营利性组织一直缺少有商业头脑的管理人。这些实体组织需要有商业天分的MBA毕业生帮助他们找到有创意的解决方法，应付

社区中的挑战。哈佛商学院的社会事业课能帮我研究非营利性组织管理中存在的问题，还能帮我拓展商业技能，同时，为我在毕业后提供专业机会。

社区服务一直是我生活中的一部分。我曾在诺克斯维尔的男孩女孩俱乐部担任导师，最近又参与了国际仁人家园和 Hands on Memphis 组织的活动。通过这些领导经历，我找到了生命中一些特别的东西，我希望让其成为我事业的一部分。

哈佛商学院的案例分析教学法，会是我与那些志同道合的同学相互沟通的宝贵机会。学生团队的多样性可以帮我通过不同的视角观察世界，拓展我处理不同问题的视野，并建立终生的友谊网。通过这些经历，我确信我会在毕业后对非营利性组织产生有意义的影响。

61
在全球化背景下与贫困斗争

I have watched the world change around people who were unprepared for its transformation. I have defined *commodity* for Brazilian coffee brokers whose market suddenly seemed to ignore them. I have argued about Mercosur with a tired finance minister in Ecuador, and have seen Dominican friends fight for jobs in a new *zona franca* condemned by international labor groups.

I want to help clarify the confusion, and I want the Harvard Business School to be my accomplice.

I am choosing HBS for the traditional outputs. I want to increase my impact on organizations, to join a network of people with the courage to reach difficult goals, to gain unmatched credibility as a messenger. HBS has an outstanding reputation for offering these things, and my research confirms it. Most of the HBS students and alumni I know are risking their definitions of greatness.

I also want the journey. I want the daily luxury of exploring the world with the extraordinary community that HBS builds. I want to engage Frances Frei on my company's failed technology dream and see Haitian competitiveness from Michael Porter's perspective. I want to argue with James Austin about the private sector's ability to drive social change and discuss the responsibilities of corporations with exceptional peers who will translate their convictions into meaningful action.

I came to on the FRONTIER to learn to fight poverty in a new global context. I want to advance that fight, and I want to test and improve my strategy at HBS, a place that will hold me to the highest standards of analysis and tutor me in the messy art of leadership.

点评

这篇充满诗意的文章在开篇就吸引了读者的注意力。申请人抛弃传统的“论点加论据”结构，巧妙地罗列了申请哈佛商学院工商硕士的理由。当然，最引人注目的依然是申请人流露出的对改变周围世界的热情。

即使申请人没有明说，甚至不用看申请人的其他几篇申请短文，读者也可以从文章中推断出申请人将继续从事经济发展活动的雄心壮志。申请人用只言片语介绍了他在新兴市场的工作，展示了他过往的经历。这些描述因为添加了申请人的个人感情色彩——与厄瓜多尔财政部长的一席谈话，多米尼加共和国的朋友们找工作等，而变得尤其有说服力。尽管申请人取得了所有这些成就，但还是表达了自己重返学校读 MBA 的愿望。

申请人列举了几个精辟的例子解释他为什么选中哈佛商学院。很明显，他做过背景调查，熟悉教授以及他们的科研领域。这一段文字还透露出他的兴趣爱好和个人动机。本文的力量不仅来自申请人高尚的目标，也来自其生动、流畅的文笔。通过申请人充分表达的信念，读者定会相信申请人将成为未来变革的主要力量。

【参考译文】

眼看着世界一点点改变，而生活在其中的人面对变化却毫无准备。我曾告诉那些似乎突然间被市场抛弃的巴西咖啡中介商什么叫作“商品”；我曾与疲惫的厄瓜多尔财政部长争论南方共同市场；我曾看见多米尼加的朋友们争取一个遭国际劳工组织谴责的新厂区的工作岗位……

我希望帮助他们理清混沌，我希望哈佛商学院助我一臂之力。

我选择哈佛商学院是为了获得传统收益。我想增强我对组织的影响力，我想认识一群有勇气追求艰难目标的人，我想成为一名先驱，拥有公信力。哈佛商学院因提供这些益处而闻名遐迩，而调查也证实了这点。我认识的大部分哈佛商学院学生和毕业生正在冒险追求他们心目中的卓越事业。

我也想要这段经历。我希望每天与哈佛商学院培养的杰出人才一起尽情探索世界。我想邀请弗朗西斯·弗赖参与我们公司失败了的科技梦；我想学着用迈克尔·波特的视角分析海地的竞争力；我想和詹姆斯·奥斯汀辩论私营经济对推动社会变革所起的作用；我还想和把信念转化成有意义的行动，和杰出人才共同讨论企业责任。

我想在前沿阵地学习如何在新的全球化背景下与贫困斗争。我想推动这场斗争，我想在哈佛商学院实践我的战略，并加以改进。哈佛商学院能教给我最理性的分析技能，指导我学习模糊的领导艺术。

OPTIONAL ESSAY

命题9
可选话题

Is there any other information that you believe would be helpful to the board in understanding you better and in considering your application? Please be concise.

你是否还有其他可以帮助录取委员会更好地了解你、审核你的申请信息？请保持简洁。

解题思路

你大概跟大部分申请人一样在怀疑“可选话题”是否真的可选择。要是其他人都写了就你没写，怎么办？可是写完了前面6篇短文，你还能写什么呢？

一系列的申请命题，其主要目的是让你尽量全面地展示个性。其他命题关注领导力、成就、个人发展，而可选话题可以给你提供一个机会，让你强调自己趣味横生的一面，或者进一步解释你的独特状况。这是一个机会，让你讲述你的追求、引导你日常生活的根本信仰，或者解释你如何投身于大学课外活动以至于GPA受到了影响。如果你还有一些有意义的事情之前没告诉我们，那么请抓住这个机会。话说回来，千万别重复。光拉长篇幅而没有真材实料，是无法提高整体的申请资质的，甚至可能因此受损。此外，如果你想解释GMAT成绩不够优秀的原因，请确保你给出的是解释而不是借口。

实际上，只有寥寥数位申请人回复可选话题。后面4篇范文展示了此话题可以探讨的范围。然而，这些文章都有个共同点：每看一篇都会让你感觉“申请人一定是个风趣的人，我很想见见他”。如果你认为你写的短文也能产生如此效果，那么一定要写。记住，你所做的一切最终都是为了使你更符合哈佛商学院MBA候选人的形象。

点评人： 帕韦尔·斯威特克

62
孩提时代的价值观

At the age of seven, I left my "kid days" of playing banker behind to open a lemonade stand on the front porch. Capitalizing on my parents' planned garage sale, I sold cold drinks and red licorice to the visiting bargain hunters. As the years passed, my ventures evolved into neighborhood car washes and a business called PUPS (personalized urban puppy sitters).

More than a young entrepreneurial instinct, I attribute my actions to the set of values I was imbued with by my parents. They succeeded in teaching me the importance of work and the value of money. While my friends received flat allowances of $20 a week, my sister and I received none. When I begged for the latest gimmicky toy, my mother said "save up your money and buy it." Sure enough, after I had saved enough to purchase a Nintendo set in the fifth grade, I was overflowing with pride. Granted, my sister and I only had enough money for one game, but we played it with relish.

At the age of eleven, I became an avid babysitter, filling my nights, weekends, and even early mornings with child-care commitments. By the time I took off for my junior year in Spain, I had enough savings to cover my personal expenses for the entire year abroad. Churros tasted sweeter and movies were more enjoyable remembering the work that afforded those luxuries.

In university, while taking full loads to complete two bachelor's degrees, I held down several part-time jobs to help support myself through college (working from fifteen to twenty-five hours per week). This, on top of holding multiple club leadership positions and squeezing in time at the gym or with friends, caused friends to question how I fit life into twenty-four-hour days. But work has never been an optional item for me. Though my parents never demanded it, they have taught me why it is indispensable. And it has made me a more independent and disciplined individual.

点评

如果本文放在其他的命题里，可能很难解释申请人如何埋头苦干、独立和自律。它的主题并不完全是一个决定性时刻，也不能简单地算作三大成就之一。然而，它却有效地说明了申请人日常遵循的职业道德及其起源。

乍一看，卖冷饮和照看小孩的故事看上去可能有点老套，但是申请人清晰地解释了这些经历如何塑造了她的个人发展。虽然她在其余的几篇 Essay 中描绘的多半是一个小有成就的年轻女商人，而本篇 Essay 却让我们了解她是如何达到那些成就的。在这个意义上，本篇 Essay 完善了她的入学申请，并使录取委员会更深入地了解了她这个人。

【参考译文】

7 岁那年，我告别了玩纸牌的“孩提时代”，在家门口摆了个卖水的小摊。利用父母安排的卖旧货的机会，我向前来淘便宜货的人兜售冷饮和红甘草汁。几年之后，我的冒险经历发展到了给邻居洗车，以及一桩称为“PUPS”（个性化的市内小狗代看）的生意。

这些行为不仅仅源于一名小企业家的本能，我将它们更多地归功于父母给我灌输的价值观。他们成功地教会了我工作的重要性和金钱的价值。我的朋友们每周能拿到固定的 20 美元零花钱，而我和妹妹却一分钱都没有。当我央求父母给我买最新上市的玩具时，妈妈回答道：“自己攒钱就可以买了！”的确，在我五年级时攒钱买了一台任天堂游戏机后，我的心中充满了自豪感。显然，我和妹妹只买得起一款游戏，但我们玩得津津有味。

11 岁时，我成了一名照看小孩的热心保姆，把我的晚上、周末，甚至清晨都投入到照看小孩的工作中。等到我去西班牙上大三时，我已经攒够了钱，可以支付自己在国外全年的开销。一想到为了购买“奢侈品”而付出的努力，西班牙油条变得更加香甜，电影也变得更加令人愉悦。

在大学里，我一边开足马力学习，完成了两个本科学位，一边做几份兼职工作（每周工作 15 ~ 25 小时不等）养活自己，再加上几个俱乐部的领导工作，还要挤时间去健身，或者与朋友出去玩，导致朋友们难以相信我是如何将这样忙碌的生活安排在 24 小时之内的。工作对我而言从来不是一个可选项，虽然父母从来没有要求我这么做，但是他们已经让我懂得了工作的重要性。这也使我成为了一个更加独立、更加自律的人。

63
幸福生活的深刻领悟

I enjoy never giving up, always thinking there's a way, and if there is not one, creating it. I enjoy walking through Central Park with Paige, my girlfriend of six years, and discovering new paths. I enjoy helping Ground Zero construction workers by cold-calling major insole distributors and organizing five hundred pairs of insoles to be donated to the Red Cross. I enjoy seeing that the elevator has not moved off my floor between the time I come home late and when I wake up early to go running the next morning.

I enjoy having close friends with not-so-close personalities, histories, goals, and lifestyles. I have friends who work at Lehman and Solomon, and another who works at her mother's Common Grounds coffee shop; I have friends who visit families on opposite sides of the Dead Sea but can still have peaceful conversations about U.S. foreign policy.

I enjoy never having a single regret, standing in the present and leaning toward the future. I enjoy making mistakes and realizing my first impression was wrong. The best manager I ever worked for initially struck me as a timid and uninspiring person. Weeks later I realized how her unthreatening nature was an incredibly powerful tool in putting clients at ease with changing their minds and with accepting her bold and innovative ideas.

I enjoy listening, learning, trying new things, and growing. I enjoy finally learning to surf Costa Rica's fifteen-foot waves after spending the better part of two days underwater. I enjoy seeing my first boss finally laugh when I built up the nerve to do an impression of her at the company Christmas party. I enjoy laughing, making people laugh, and people that can laugh at themselves.

I enjoy how my family's diversity has shaped me. My younger brother, who spent time in three different high schools, is beginning to act on my coaching that straightening up his act does not mean living an uninteresting life. While my father grew up playing stickball on the streets of Queens, N.Y., my mother learned how to sail her father's boat in the Lake of Lucerne in Switzerland. I enjoy my parents' different renditions of my childhood. I enjoy knowing that my personality lies, like the truth in their contrasting tales, somewhere in between.

点评

作为一篇打算用生活经历充实商学院申请的文章，本文堪称力作。每一句都传达了申请人崭新的一面——兴趣、情感、爱好、文化认同。他对生活永不知足的劲头不容忽视。这份似乎永无止境的经历清单，一旦拼成整体，就能绘出一个丰富多彩、活泼有趣的人。文章谦虚朴实，而申请人的诚实立刻博得了人们的信任。

本文正如前面一篇，大大增加了申请材料的深度。这位有紧迫感的银行经纪人变成了一位拥有宽广平和的世界观的申请人，他不仅可以带给 MBA 课堂一套理财技能，还能带来他对幸福生活的深刻领悟。

【参考译文】

我欣赏永不放弃的精神，坚信凡事总有解决方法，若没有，那就想方法解决。我享受和交往了 6 年的女朋友佩吉穿越中央公园，感受探索新路径的乐趣。我喜欢以陌生人的身份致电大型鞋垫分销商，从而帮助重建世贸大厦的工人，并将募集到的 500 双鞋垫捐给红十字会。我喜欢深夜到家直到次日早起晨跑时，看见电梯一直停留在我家的楼层。

我乐意结交一群性格特征、生活经历、人生目标以及生活方式不尽相同的好朋友。有的朋友在雷曼公司和所罗门公司上班，有的在帮母亲打理“共同基

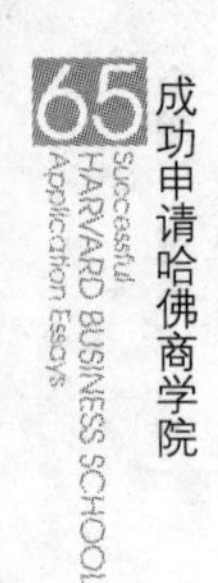

石”咖啡馆；我有个朋友曾拜访过住在死海对面的家庭，但仍然可以平静地谈论美国的外交政策。

我欣赏凡事不留遗憾的态度，身处现在，展望将来。我乐意尝试错误，且乐意承认不能光凭第一印象取人。迄今为止我所遇到的最好的经理，在一开始给我的印象是一个胆小怕事又死气沉沉的人。几周后，我发现她那平易近人的个性如此令人不可思议，能够使客户轻松改变主意，接受她的大胆创新。

我喜欢倾听、学习、尝试新鲜事物，并随之成长。我花了两天时间潜水，最终还学会了在哥斯达黎加高达 5 米的浪头上冲浪。我欣赏自己在公司的圣诞晚会上鼓起勇气模仿我的第一任老板，她终于笑出声来。我喜欢笑，喜欢逗别人笑，喜欢那些开得起玩笑的人。

我感激多样化的家庭造就了我的性格。弟弟转了三所高中，现在开始遵从我的教导。我告诉他，收敛行为并不意味着过无聊的生活。父亲在纽约皇后区玩棍子球长大，与此同时，母亲正在瑞士的卢塞恩湖上学习驾驭他父亲的船。我喜欢聆听父母对我的童年生活的不同演绎。我欣赏自己的性格介于中间的某一点，正如他们所讲的自相矛盾的故事中存在的真相一样。

64
中国汉字的博大精深

Their dramatic peaks and graceful curves speak volumes.

Chinese characters are expressive, beautiful, deep. Chinese "words" are pictures of ideas, communicating a concept as both what it is and is not. For instance, the character for man joins a farmer's field with an arm of strength; to the Chinese, a male without vocation is not truly a man. My life is not just about who I am, but also who I am not. Back in high school, I was an accomplished cellist. But I harbored no illusions about music as a profession, and college life beckoned for my time. I am no longer that cellist; recently, as I played in a trio for a wedding, the violinist repeatedly winced at my good intentions.

Halfway through college, I found myself envying my roommate for his drawing class assignments—I was starving for creative expression. After tasting southern China during a summer Christian mission, I registered for a Chinese class. I was forewarned by Chinese friends who had taken Mandarin at Duke: they, from Chinese-language homes, could barely handle the workload… why should I, lacking Chinese background, risk my schedule or my transcript? But life encompasses not just what I choose, but also what I avoid. How could I retreat from the challenge of Chinese before the first day of class?

My three semesters of Chinese were a delight. For hours at a stretch, I hid in the library to write characters, millennia of culture and wisdom flowing through my hand.

I chose to embrace the beauty, expression, and depth of the Chinese language, and the fruit of my choice has become a part of me.

点评

前面那篇范文展现的阅历几乎令人目不暇接，而该申请人却集中讲述他的一个兴趣。不过，本篇 Essay 的重点并非在于他努力学习中文、练习书法，而在于他勇于迎接生活中的挑战这个富有哲理的问题。这些轶事表明，申请人有能力决定哪些事情在生活中不值得一搏。全文贯穿着一种深刻的自我意识，并含蓄地证明了申请人的成熟和稳健。

或许，本篇 Essay 在你看来与商业毫无关联。然而，申请人的自我反省能力很可能在今后帮助他在企业中作决策。申请人用一种十分微妙的手法强化了他作为一名称职的未来商界领袖的形象。

【参考译文】

汉字生动的折钩和优雅的弧度都意味深长。

中国的汉字富有表现力，美丽而深奥。中国汉字是思想的图画，同时传达着“是”与“不是”的概念。举个例子，“男”这个字是农田和臂力的组合。对中国人来说，没有事业的男人不是真正的男人。我的生活不仅仅关乎我是谁，同时也关乎我不是谁。读高中时，我曾是一个小有成就的大提琴手。但是，我并不幻想将音乐作为我的职业，大学生活在向我招手。我已经不再是那个大提琴手了。最近，我在一个婚礼上参加了一场三重奏表演，但那位小提琴手却因我的好意而一再打退堂鼓。

大学生活过半的时候，我发现自己非常羡慕室友的画图课作业——我正渴望获得一种充满创意的表达方式。一次暑期的基督教宣教之旅，让我体验了一回中国南方的生活，之后我就报了中文课。有几位之前在杜克大学上过中文普通话课的华人朋友事先警告我说，他们来自说汉语的家庭尚且很难应付课程的作业量……我这样没有中文背景的人为什么要冒这种可能影响我学习进度和成绩的风险呢？然而，人生不仅包括我选择的东西，还包括我逃避的东西。在我上第一堂课之前，怎么可以在中文的挑战面前退缩呢？

三个学期的中文课是一段愉悦的经历。我曾躲在图书馆，连着几个小时书写汉字，几千年来的文化与智慧就在我的手下流淌而过。

我选择去体会中国语言的华美、深奥和表现力，而这个选择的成果已经成了我个人生活的一部分。

65
对“个人社会责任”的深度思考

I believe it would be helpful for the board if I could share my vision of "social responsibility of individuals."

I believe everyone has the responsibility of putting his/her personal and professional skills to the benefit of the society he/she lives in. To work on behalf of society is to invest in people believing one can make the difference both in the present and in the future world. This responsibility stems from the fact that what we are today has been the product of other people's past investment.

Throughout my life I've always tried to make the difference in my community. I've led a Catholic informal training and development organization for youth, I've visited an orphans' house once a week for a year striving to help them in their personal development, and I've created and currently lead the choir of my community Sunday mass. This is unusual in Portugal since in this country, unlike in the United States, participating in community activities is not a part of common individuals' lives.

I intend to keep on using my skills and forces on community service, either on my free time or while working.

Because of my interest in social activities I admire HBS involvement in social enterprise. Its elective courses, like effective leadership of social enterprises and entrepreneurship in the social sector, its Volunteer Consulting Organization and Social Enterprise Club would make it easier for someone like me to be actively involved in social enterprises activities throughout my life.

点评

申请人利用可选话题分享了一个非常有力的想法——个人的社会责任。尽管很容易被人看作教条主义，但是他成功地向读者展现了推动他生活的力量。为了避免文章过于抽象和不切实际，申请人用参与社区活动的具体事例来表现他的信念。

本文是利用可选话题增强申请竞争力的一个很好的例子。申请人把自己对社区服务的投入与哈佛商学院的社会企业计划以及志愿咨询机构联系在一起。结果是，他不仅表明自己非常熟悉哈佛商学院，而且价值观与哈佛商学院非常吻合，这使他成为“天生的”候选人。

【参考译文】

我相信，分享我对“个人社会责任”的看法将有助于录取委员会了解我。

我相信，每个人都有责任运用自己的个人能力和职业技能改善所处的社会环境。改造社会，就是在自认能够改变现实和未来世界的人身上投资。个人的社会责任来自这个事实——我们今日所有乃是前人投资的产物。

我的一生都致力于改善我现在生活的社区。组织青年天主教非正式培训发展组织；曾在一年中每周探望孤儿院一次，帮助他们个人成长；组建社区周日聚会的合唱团，而且最近我还开始领唱。这在葡萄牙是非同寻常的，因为这里不比美国，参与社区活动不是大家生活的一部分。

我愿意在闲暇时光，甚至是工作时间，继续尽我所能地服务社区。

由于对社会活动的浓厚兴趣，我很欣赏哈佛商学院对社会事业的参与。它的选修课程，比如公共事业的有效领导和社会公益创投，以及志愿咨询机构、社会企业俱乐部，都会帮助像我这样的人更加积极地投身于社会企业活动中。

65

Successful

HARVARD BUSINESS SCHOOL

Application Essays

译者后记

2012 年，武汉大学老校长刘道玉召集了一场“理想大学专题研讨会”。参加本次会议的嘉宾大多是教育界有影响的专家和学者，而北京大学钱理群教授在会上的一番话更是引发了微博上的一场热议。

“我们的一些大学，包括北京大学，正在培养一些‘精致的利己主义者’，他们高智商、世俗、老道、善于表演、懂得配合，更善于利用体制达到自己的目的。这种人一旦掌握权力，比一般的贪官污吏危害更大。”钱理群教授说道。这俨然是对中国高等教育最严酷的宣判。大学本该是一片净土，是理想主义者的家园，如今却正在被功利主义、浮躁的社会风气所荼毒。

让我们回头再来看看哈佛商学院。经管院校大约是大学里最“铜臭”的地方，因为它培养的是追逐利益最大化的商界精英。可是从这 65 篇经典 Essay 中，我们看到的却是一个又一个性格鲜明、怀抱梦想的年轻人。有的人热心服侍弱势群体、孤儿、低收入的亚裔美国妇女和流离他乡的移民等；有的人出于纯粹的兴趣，笔耕不辍；有的人为了追逐心中的理想放弃丰厚的收入……每一个人都是那么真实，又是那么精彩！

读者大可以把本书看成是又一本急功近利的“宝典”或“秘笈”，帮你敲开顶尖商学院的大门，正如网上诸多广为流传的大公司“面试圣经”。或者，也可以借着此书停下来，真正思索一回人生。

本书的引进源于我的恩师孙路弘的极力推荐，并交托给我翻译，感谢他一贯以来的信任。翻译的过程也是我学习的过程，艰苦而美好。另外，要感谢我的爱人赵周、家人张夏林和支菊芬，他们实实在在的支持才能让我在照顾两个孩子之余，仍能挤出时间完成本书的翻译工作。还要感谢的是苏雪菲和黄理明等朋友在这个过程中提供的莫大帮助。

由于译者水平有限，或者一时的疏忽造成的错译、漏译，敬请读者批评、指正。如果您有心得愿意分享，也请一定联系我。我的 e-mail 是 zhangkeli@gmail.com。

湛庐，与思想有关……

如何阅读商业图书

商业图书与其他类型的图书，由于阅读目的和方式的不同，因此有其特定的阅读原则和阅读方法，先从一本书开始尝试，再熟练应用。

阅读原则1 二八原则

对商业图书来说，80%的精华价值可能仅占20%的页码。要根据自己的阅读能力，进行阅读时间的分配。

阅读原则2 集中优势精力原则

在一个特定的时间段内，集中突破20%的精华内容。也可以在一个时间段内，集中攻克一个主题的阅读。

阅读原则3 递进原则

高效率的阅读并不一定要按照页码顺序展开，可以挑选自己感兴趣的部分阅读，再从兴趣点扩展到其他部分。阅读商业图书切忌贪多，从一个小主题开始，先培养自己的阅读能力，了解文字风格、观点阐述以及案例描述的方法，目的在于对方法的掌握，这才是最重要的。

阅读原则4 好为人师原则

在朋友圈中主导、控制话题，引导话题向自己设计的方向去发展，可以让读书收获更加扎实、实用、有效。

阅读方法与阅读习惯的养成

（1）回想。阅读商业图书常常不会一口气读完，第二次拿起书时，至少用15分钟回想上次阅读的内容，不要翻看，实在想不起来再翻看。严格训练自己，一定要回想，坚持50次，会逐渐养成习惯。

（2）做笔记。不要试图让笔记具有很强的逻辑性和系统性，不需要有深刻的见解和思想，只要是文字，就是对大脑的锻炼。在空白处多写多画，随笔、符号、涂色、书签、便签、折页，甚至拆书都可以。

（3）读后感和PPT。坚持写读后感可以大幅度提高阅读能力，做PPT可以提高逻辑分析能力。从写读后感开始，写上5篇以后，再尝试做PPT。连续做上5个PPT，再重复写三次读后感。如此坚持，阅读能力将会大幅度提高。

（4）思想的超越。要养成上述阅读习惯，通常需要6个月的严格训练，至少完成4本书的阅读。你会慢慢发现，自己的思想开始跳脱出来，开始有了超越作者的感觉。比拟作者、超越作者、试图凌驾于作者之上思考问题，是阅读能力提高的必然结果。

好的方法其实很简单，难就难在执行。需要毅力、执著、长期的坚持，从而养成习惯。用心学习，就会得到心的改变、思想的改变。阅读，与思想有关。

[特别感谢：营销及销售行为专家 孙路弘 智慧支持！]

我们出版的所有图书，封底和前勒口都有“湛庐文化”的标志

并归于两个品牌

找“小红帽”

为了便于读者在浩如烟海的书架陈列中清楚地找到湛庐，我们在每本图书的封面左上角，以及书脊上部 47mm 处，以红色作为标记——称之为**“小红帽”**。同时，封面左上角标记**“湛庐文化 Slogan”**，书脊上标记**“湛庐文化 Logo”**，且下方标注图书所属品牌。

湛庐文化主力打造两个品牌：**财富汇**，致力于为商界人士提供国内外优秀的经济管理类图书；**心视界**，旨在通过心理学大师、心灵导师的专业指导为读者提供改善生活和心境的通路。

阅读的最大成本

读者在选购图书的时候，往往把成本支出的焦点放在书价上，其实不然。

时间才是读者付出的最大阅读成本。

阅读的时间成本=选择花费的时间+阅读花费的时间+误读浪费的时间

湛庐希望成为一个“与思想有关”的组织，成为中国与世界思想交汇的聚集地。通过我们的工作和努力，潜移默化地改变中国人、商业组织的思维方式，与世界先进的理念接轨，帮助国内的企业和经理人，融入世界，这是我们的使命和价值。

我们知道，这项工作就像跑马拉松，是极其漫长和艰苦的。但是我们有决心和毅力去不断推动，在朝着我们目标前进的道路上，所有人都是同行者和推动者。希望更多的专家、学者、读者一起来加入我们的队伍，在当下改变未来。

湛庐文化2008-2012年获奖书目

《正能量》

《新智囊》2012年经管类十大图书，京东2012好书榜年度新书。

35年职业经理人养成心得，写给有追求的职场人。

聆听总裁的职场故事，发掘自己与生俱来的正能量。

《牛奶可乐经济学》

国家图书馆“第四届文津奖”十本获奖图书之一，唯一获奖的商业类图书。

搜狐、《第一财经日报》2008年十本最佳商业图书。

用经济学的眼光看待生活和工作，体验作为“经济学家”的美妙之处。

《清单革命》

《中国图书商报》商业类十大好书。

全球思想家正在读的20本书之一。

一场应对复杂世界的观念变革，一部捍卫安全与正确的实践宣言。

《大而不倒》

《金融时报》·高盛2010年度最佳商业图书入选作品。

美国《外交政策》杂志评选的全球思想家正在阅读的20本书之一。

蓝狮子·新浪2010年度十大最佳商业图书，《智囊悦读》2010年度十大最具价值经管图书。

一部金融界的《2012》，一部丹·布朗式的鸿篇巨制。

《金融之王》

《金融时报》·高盛2010年度最佳商业图书。

蓝狮子2011年度十大最佳商业图书，《第一财经日报》2011年度十大金融投资书籍。

一部优美的人物传记，一部独特视角的经济金融史。

《快乐竞争力》

蓝狮子2012年度十大最佳商业图书。

赢得优势的7个积极心理学法则，全美10大幸福企业“幸福感”培训专用书。

《大客户销售》

蓝狮子·新营销2012最佳营销商业图书。

著名营销及销售行为专家孙路弘最新作品，一本提升大客户销售能力的实战秘笈。

《自营销》

百道网2013年度潜力新书。

全球最具创意广告公司CP+B掌门人的洞见之作，让好产品和好营销同唱一首歌。

《认知盈余》

2011年度和讯华文财经图书大奖。

看“互联网革命最伟大的思考者”克莱·舍基如何开启无组织的时间力量。

看自由时间如何成就“有闲”世界，如何引领“有闲”经济与“有闲”商业的未来。

《爆发》

百道网2013年度潜力新书。

大数据时代预见未来的新思维，颠覆《黑天鹅》的惊世之作，揭开人类行为背后隐藏的模式。

《微力无边》

2011年度和讯华文财经图书大奖“最佳装帧设计奖”。

中国最早的社会化媒体营销研究者杜子建首部作品，一部微博前传，半部营销后传。

《神话的力量》

《心理月刊》2011年度最佳图书奖。

在诸神与英雄的世界中发现自我，当代神话学大师约瑟夫·坎贝尔毕生精髓之作。

《真实的幸福》

《职场》2010年度最具阅读价值的10本职场书籍。

积极心理学之父马丁·塞利格曼扛鼎之作。

哈佛最吸引人、最受欢迎的幸福课。

延伸阅读

《超级合作者》

◎ 新时代的“达尔文”马丁·诺瓦克创立第3进化原则，洞悉人类社会与行为的里程碑式著作。

◎ 著名经济学家、北京大学教授汪丁丁鼎力推荐。

《企鹅与怪兽》

◎ 合作，互联时代的下一个大趋势。继《人人时代》《认知盈余》后最值得关注的颠覆之作。

◎ 腾讯公司高级执行副总裁汤道生、洞察中国社会数字化第一人胡泳、浙江大学教授叶航专文推荐。

《管理百年（珍藏版）》

◎ 一本书，梳理百年管理变迁，洞悉未来管理趋势。这不仅是一部现代管理学史，更是一部现代商业进化史。

◎ 管理思潮发源地《哈佛商业评论》，国内三大顶尖商学院（北大、清华、上海交大）鼎力推荐。

◎ 全球最具影响力的50大思想家（Thinkers 50）创始人经典作品。

殿堂级管理大师亨利·明茨伯格作品典藏（珍藏版）（套装共2册）

◎ 当今世界上最杰出的管理思想家明茨伯格最知名作品再版升级；《管理工作的本质》是明茨伯格的第一本著作，是经理角色管理学派最早出版的经典著作。《卓有成效的组织》是明茨伯格的得意之作，管理者打造卓越组织必须聆听的声音。

◎ 与德鲁克齐名的管理大师明茨伯格最得意作品，MBA、EMBA导师级读物。

◎ 精装再版，湛庐独家策划阅读地图，呈现最优阅读体验。

65 SUCCESSFUL HARVARD BUSINESS SCHOOL APPLICATION ESSAYS: THE STAFF OF THE HARBUS, THE HARVARD BUSINESS SCHOOL STUDENT NEWSPAPER
by DAN ERCK, PAVEL SWIATEK

This edition arranged with ST.MARTIN'S PRESS, LLC. through Big Apple Tuttle-Mori Agency, Inc., Labuan, Malaysia.

图书在版编目（CIP）数据

成功申请哈佛商学院：经典 Essay65 篇 /（美）埃尔克，（美）斯威特克，哈佛商学院 *Harbus* 编辑部编；张科丽译．—杭州：浙江人民出版社，2014.5

ISBN 978-7-213-06045-8

Ⅰ.①成… Ⅱ.①埃… ②斯… ③哈… ④张… Ⅲ.①英语－写作 Ⅳ.①H315

中国版本图书馆 CIP 数据核字（2014）第 063710 号

浙江省版权局
著作权合同登记章
图字:11-2014-68 号

上架指导：管理 /MBA 与工商管理

成功申请哈佛商学院：经典Essay65篇

作　　者：［美］丹·埃尔克　帕韦尔·斯威特克　哈佛商学院 *Harbus* 编辑部　编

译　　者：张科丽　译

出版发行：浙江人民出版社（杭州体育场路347号　邮编　310006）

市场部电话：（0571）85061682　85176516

集团网址：浙江出版联合集团　http://www.zjcb.com

责任编辑：朱丽芳

责任校对：朱　妍

印　　刷：藁城市京瑞印刷有限公司

开　　本：720 mm × 965 mm 1/16　　**印　　张：**15.5

字　　数：24.3 万　　**插　　页：**1

版　　次：2014 年 5 月第 1 版　　**印　　次：**2014 年 5 月第 1 次印刷

书　　号：ISBN 978-7-213-06045-8

定　　价：45.90 元